"The foundations of law and order have collapsed. What can the righteous do?" the Psalmist asked.

In these pages you will journey with a household of faith through "one of the heaviest moments of human history"— the Rwandan genocide of 1994.

Chris Karuhije and his family escaped the slaughter that took over a million lives in 100 days of horror. When I interviewed him on national television in 2008, I expected an oppressive return to that atrocity.

But like the author, this stirring testimony radiates Jesus! "We weren't saved for nothing" Chris boldly declared, on 100 Huntley Street.

The book I knew he would write is right on time with the troubled and uncertain world we are facing today. Royal encouragement awaits!

—Moira Brown, co-host of 100 Huntley Street, Canada's longest daily talk show and one of Canada's top 100 Christian Women Leaders.

We Were Royal Refugees

How One Family Survived the
Mass Slaughter in Rwanda

CHRIS KARUHIJE

WE WERE ROYAL REFUGEES
Copyright © 2018 by Chris Karuhije

All rights reserved. Neither this publication nor any part of this publication may be reproduced or transmitted in any form or by any means, electronic or mechanical, including photocopying, recording or any information storage and retrieval system, without permission in writing from the author.

Viewpoints expressed within this book are that of the author and do not necessarily reflect the viewpoints of Word Alive Press.

Scripture quotations are from The Holy Bible, English Standard Version® (ESV®), copyright © 2001 by Crossway, a publishing ministry of Good News Publishers. Used by permission. All rights reserved.

Printed in Canada

ISBN: 978-1-4866-1561-2

Word Alive Press
119 De Baets Street Winnipeg, MB R2J 3R9
www.wordalivepress.ca

Cataloguing in Publication information can be obtained from Library and Archives Canada.

contents

PROLOGUE	vii
INTRODUCTION	xi
CHAPTER 1: WINDS OF DESTRUCTION	1
CHAPTER 2: EXODUS	7
CHAPTER 3: A NEW BEGINNING	23
CHAPTER 4: LOVE STORY	33
CHAPTER 5: THE CHAINING OF RWANDA'S SOUL	43
CHAPTER 6: LIGHT IN THE DARKNESS	51
CHAPTER 7: THE GREAT ESCAPE	61
CHAPTER 8: THE WALKING DEAD	71
CHAPTER 9: KINGDOM ABOVE THE CLOUDS	83
CHAPTER 10: THE END AND THE BEGINNING	97

Prologue

ALPHONSE SHOOK THE DUST OFF HIS CLOTHES AND WIPED THE BLOOD off his face. It wasn't his blood. It belonged to the body that lay lifeless on the bloodstained floor beside him. Many more bodies surrounded him, silent and still. The echoes of their scream no longer rang through the little neighbourhood, though they still rang loud and clear in Alphonse's head.

This was in a suburb of Kigali, Rwanda's capital city. Several feet behind Alphonse was a large hole that had become a makeshift burial ground for the many bodies that lay within. It wouldn't be long before he was part of it. No one would be able to find his body, let alone identify it.

Time stood still, and the world fell silent for what seemed like hours but was mere seconds in reality.

"Look at me!" Alphonse raised his eyes to face the man who screamed at him, only to face the barrel of an AK-47 pointed right at him. The wielder was a member of the Interahamwe—the feared militia that had been seeking him for weeks. He was not the only soldier there. Many more were disposing of the slain bodies and searching for any Tutsis hiding in the brush and abandoned homes.

Behind this scene sat the massive Anglican cathedral where Alphonse had been the pastor for years. Inside, the Interahamwe had desecrated the sanctuary by murdering civilians and leaving their mutilated carcasses to rot. They had brought some people out of the church building and executed them on the church steps. The Hutu *Interahamwe*—meaning "those that fight together" in Kinyarwanda, the official language of Rwanda—was a militia united by a common hate for the Tutsi people. For years they trained in secrecy, enjoying the backing of the Hutu-led government, being fed lies and deceit regarding the Tutsi people and anticipating the time when they would wreak havoc on the *inyenzi*, the "cockroaches." When the right time came, they emerged from their secret facilities and hidden forests like bats out of hell, roaming from village to village, city to city, sawing and hacking everyone in their path who was Tutsi or politically moderate Hutu. Their battle songs preceded them, and the clanging of their machetes struck fear in all who heard it. They wanted to not only kill but also torture, and severed limbs, decapitated bodies, and blood lay scattered in their wake. They would later be called *abantu bapfuye bahagaze,* men who are dead yet stand—zombies.

The man shouted insults and expletives at Alphonse, but they flew past him. He realized that these were his last moments on earth, and fear paralyzed his body and deafened him. It clung to him and tightened around his insides like vise grip. Memories of his five children—Patrick, Charity, Benjamin, Christopher, and baby David—poured into his mind like an avalanche. It had been two months since he last saw them. They would not be able to give him a proper burial or find out what had happened to him. He had left in haste and against Thacienne's pleading.

Thacienne—there was a name that brought a lump to his throat and tears to his eyes. *My Thacienne, what's going to happen to you?* If there had been a bleaker time in his life, Alphonse could not think of it.

Then it came. *What is this?* A peace like soft rain descended upon his heart and mind. It was almost tangible. He could feel fear lose its grip, and—could it be? Was this joy he felt? No, it could not be a feeling, not his, anyway. It was as if an artesian well was bubbling up from within him.

"Look at me, you filth!" Bursting with hate, the man spat in Alphonse's face. He hit him with the blunt end of his assault rifle, sending Alphonse staggering back. In pain, Alphonse let out a cry. The rifle had created a cut above his right eye. Blood gushed out, but Alphonse gathered himself and faced the man. Joy and peace continued to spring forth from the well, drowning the fear.

The Bible says that the young evangelist Stephen, the first martyr, gazed into heaven itself and saw a kingdom above the clouds (Acts 7:55-56). Jesus was seated beside the Father. And it was with that divine vision that Stephen passed from life to glorious life in that kingdom. As the old hymn "Turn Your Eyes Upon Jesus" says, "And the things of earth will grow strangely dim in the light of His glory and grace." From reports of his departure, I believe that Alphonse, my father, had a similar experience. For with the look becoming of a man whose pilgrimage had ended, he spoke the last words he would speak on this planet: "Hurry up, for the angels are waiting. We must not let them wait."

The man squeezed the trigger.

Introduction
A FATHER AND HIS KINGDOM

DEAR LONDON AND KYLEIGH,

When I was little, my parents used to tell me a story that helped me understand why bad things happen in the world. The story was of a Father King who had a vast kingdom that stretched from infinity to infinity. The King had everything you can think of or imagine—in fact, some things you could not imagine. Countless royal subjects obeyed in whatever task or assignment they were given to do. He was the most powerful being in the universe! Yet there was a desire that the King had that no subject could fulfill and nothing in His kingdom could satisfy.

You see, deep in the heart of the Father, He saw a family, a people that were not subjects but sons and daughters. Children He could communicate with and express His love to. So the Father King went to work creating a place where this family would live. Deep in the vastness of His kingdom, shrouded in space and time, He saw the perfect place—a small round planet. He went to work right away, making it perfect. He made a beautiful garden full of animals, plants, water, and even gold and other precious stones, and He called the garden Eden.

After it was all ready, He brought forth what His heart had wanted all along. He named them Adam and Eve, and to them He gave them rulership and governance of the earth as long as they obeyed one simple command. If they turned their back on the Father in disobedience, they would make the choice to live without Him and the covering of His kingdom.

But there was an enemy.

His name was Lucifer, and he had been expelled from the Father's kingdom for treason. In pride and arrogance, he had convinced a number of subjects to attempt a coup against the Father. He, along with his minions, then awaited a time when they could strike back. They found their opportunity in the newly formed family.

Lucifer deceived the woman, and the woman convinced the man, and together they did the one thing they were commanded not to do. When the Father came down to see His children, they ran away in fear, knowing what they had done. The Father was displeased. Not only had they disobeyed Him; they had also opened the door for another kingdom to come into earth. For by convincing Adam and Eve to obey him and not the Father, Lucifer had executed the coup he had hoped to achieve long before, as they had effectively surrendered themselves to him. That day, sin and evil came into the world.

Bad things do happen in our world. But my parents also told me that when we pray, God hears our prayers and answers. I am so grateful for this story now because it prepared us for your arrival in our world. Your birth was...complicated.

"MOMO"

As the technician was looking for you at our second ultrasound, our hearts were beating quickly, but we waited patiently to hear three words: "It's a girl." The technician never said them. Instead she said, "Did you guys know that you're having twins?"

I'm not going to lie—it took a while to settle in. But when it finally did, we were beyond excited. It was perplexing that the first ultrasound missed that there were two babies, but we didn't care. We could not have prayed a better prayer or uttered a more wonderful wish. We had hoped for one girl, and God had given us two! We took pictures and told close friends and family, but before we had time to fully celebrate, we received an urgent call from our doctor. What she told us changed our world.

You see, you were specially made—there are very few like you. Our doctor told us that you are monoamniotic-monochorionic twins ("momo"), very rare and very delicate. In fact, you only come around once in every 30,000 pregnancies. But because of how special you are, how you came out was very important. In most cases, twin babies have their own placentas and sacs. Rarer still are babies with one placenta but two sacs. You were created sharing one placenta and one sac. So as you grew bigger and stronger towards your delivery date, it would be easy for your umbilical cords to get entangled, causing knots and restricting full nourishment from making it through. "If that ever happened," the doctor said, "you could have a still birth." In other words, we would give birth to a dead baby. She did not mince words. "There is a greater risk for miscarriage, and we will not be able to guarantee that the babies will make it. In fact, there is a 70 percent chance they won't make it." She looked us in the eyes and said, "Termination is an option that is on the table." It was not an option for us.

You were 21 weeks old then. Five weeks later, you were born. We would wait 69 days to see your full faces—because of the CPAP mask and feeding tube, 86 days to hear your cries, and 113 long days to bring you home. Yet even when things looked bleak and hopeless, we felt the faithful eyes of the Father in His kingdom watching over you, the same Father my parents told me about when I was little. That is why I want to share this story with you, that you may know Him.

My parents did not stay long on the earth. Your grandpa went to heaven when I was nine years old, and your grandma twenty-one years later. Before she passed on, she left me one of the greatest gifts that I could have received from her. It's this gift that I now pass on to you, your story. Even in her last moments on earth, she was telling it to me; in fact, I remember one of the last moments I spent with her.

It was in the evening, and she sat staring wearily outside the window at the setting sun that had now cast a reddish glow upon the downtown Winnipeg skyline. Part of the Canadian Museum of Human Rights, a spectacular, futuristic building, was visible from the large glass window and had been a perfect backdrop for our conversation about our tremendous escape from the clutches of violence in a small unknown country in Africa. Her tired eyes stared into my fascinated ones as I asked her question after question about our daring journey through the poisoned land of Rwanda, and raising her eyes to the ceiling, she relieved the entire episode in her mind, her white teeth showing as she smiled.

In the background, the soft humming of the monitor was interrupted by a piercing beeping indicating that her total parenteral nutrition was running low. She carefully got up and meandered to her bed, shuffling her feet as if clutching an invisible walker, and gently lowered her body to sit. She slowly peeled off the slippers that had given her warmth from the cold hospital floor and gingerly leaned back in the cot. Breathing a little faster from the activity, she lowered her head onto the pillow, slowly raised her eyes to meet mine, and with a smile quietly said, "God is good."

Her hand was resting on her bloated stomach. A few inches below that hand, buried inside her belly, sat the reason for her brokenness: a cancerous diffuse large B-cell lymphoma in its fourth stage. This was in July. In September she would begin chemotherapy treatments to shrink the tumour. By November, all treatment would be halted, it having had no effect. The TPN, her only source of nourishment, all others having failed, would start to ravage her liver, causing heavy internal bleeding. After that her kidneys would begin to shut down.

Your grandmother, Thacienne, was only fifty-eight, but because of the disease she looked much older, a far cry from the youthful woman who had defied death and lived to tell about it, which is all her body allowed her to do. Yet that youthfulness and life stood reserved inside her soul and spirit and occasionally brimmed through her eyes. "God is good," she said again, and she began to tell the stories I had grown to love, the stories I now pass on to you, my sweet daughters.

Chapter 1
WINDS OF DESTRUCTION

SHE WAS FIVE YEARS OLD AND STOOD PARALYZED, WATCHING THE scene unfold before her as if it was a dream she could not wake up from. She could hear her mother's faint and distant voice calling out to her, but her eyes remained fixed on the nightmarish event. Before her, terrified men, women, and children were fleeing from their homes, taking with them anything they could carry. Houses and huts were on fire, and thieves and hooligans with machetes and sticks ran into homes, looting and pillaging as women were dragged into the bush screaming, their abandoned babies weeping.

The little village in the Northern Province of Rwanda had been turned upside down. Musanze district, her home, was crowned as Rwanda's most mountainous region and the gateway to Volcanoes National Park, the renowned haven of the mountain gorillas. It was a beautiful land close to the twin lakes of Lake

Burera and Lake Ruhondo and a sea of banana plantations. But today, hell had descended upon it.

Amidst the chaos, Thacienne's attention was consumed by the one scene before her. Her little house, which more resembled a hut, was engulfed in flames. The thatched roof was being swallowed by the giant flame, the thin wooden beams that held it having given way. As Thacienne watched, it finally caved in, and the fire poured through the modest home, devouring whatever was left inside with a belch of smoke. The only place she had ever lived was turning into ash, with dark smoke ascending into the heavens. Although the entire majority Tutsi village was being razed to the ground, from her vantage point her whole world as she knew it was evaporating before her eyes.

"Thacy! Now!" The bellow of her father snapped her to attention, and with a last glance at the ashen pile, she ran into her father's arms, her eyes finally giving way to a rush of tears. The calloused strong hands of her father wiped her tears and picked her up, and he reassured her that all would be well. Leaving the screaming and helpless pleas behind, the Mukaminega family of nine faced the rough forests of the Musanze wilderness and began their exodus into uncertainty.

This was Rwanda circa 1959. The country's monarchy, led by a Tutsi *mwami*, a Rwandese king, was in the process of being dissolved and would be replaced by a Hutu-led republic. The beating of a Hutu minority government leader, Dominique Mbonyumutwa, sparked off a bloody revolution that stained Rwanda's soil with the blood of thousands of Tutsis in what came to be known as the Wind of Destruction, Rwanda's revolution. As many as 100,000 men, women, and children were murdered, and the Tutsis who survived the slaughter fled for their lives. By the end of the revolution, a third of the Tutsi population was displaced in neighbouring countries: Tanzania, Burundi, Uganda, and Zaire, the modern-day Republic of Congo.

Your grandmother and her family had been fortunate to dodge the winds of destruction that had blown through their village, but what they would do next was a question that not even Anastase, the patriarch of the Mukaminega family and your great-grandfather, could figure out. He was a tall, strong man who carried the respect of his wife, Bernadette, and the love of his seven children: Jean-Baptiste, Euphrasie, Dancila, Augustin, Thacienne, Bonifribe, and Anakleti.

He had managed to create a livelihood and provide for his family by working the productive Rwandan soil, and although he had received many threats from neighbouring Hutus, who taunted and ridiculed him for being Tutsi, he carried himself with honour and dignity and shrugged off their remarks as ignorance. Yet as he looked upon the tear-covered black faces of his children and the terrified eyes of his wife, Anastase realized that this was an entirely different situation. Years of threats and taunts had finally materialized into something very real, and the realization that they could die hit him like a rock. If the Hutu rebels who now ruled the lands and asserted their strength though murder and pillaging didn't kill them, hunger and the hot African sun would be obliged to.

DARKNESS FALLS

Night fell, and Anastase knew that if they did not find shelter they would be overwhelmed by wild beasts in the jungles. They finally arrived at their destination, Musanze Caves, an impressive network of over fifty caves. Stories are told of a local king who was about to be captured and hit the ground with a magical stick, forming the impressive underground tunnel systems to elude his captors in. Legend gives way to more accurate history in which we find that they were a result of volcanic eruptions. Over 2 km long, with more than thirty entrances, Musanze Caves would be a suitable retreat for the fleeing family.

As they entered they could see that they were not the only ones to have that idea. Flickering lights and distant voices signalled that more refugees were inside, perhaps a conformation of the authenticity of the plan. The howling of hyenas filled the forest every night, but Anastase encouraged her children to sleep and not fear the deep darkness of the cavern and the shrieking of the hundreds of bats above.

This would be their home for seven days. During the day, Hutu militia patrolled the area, looking for any Tutsis who had escaped. At times some wandered into the cave, seeking signs of refugees, but Thacienne and her family remained hidden in dark crevices and avoided detection. Sticks and wood were needed to burn for warmth against the wet algae-covered cave floor, but discretion was everything. Anastase joined the other heads of families in the caves in scoping out paths and exits from the enormous caves so that they could leave undetected. Their only way of escape lay in the cover of the deep darkness of the African night, but each time they ventured out they were greeted by the harrowing sounds of the jungle nightlife. Anastase was able to convince friendly Hutu families close by to smuggle cooked potatoes and beans into the cave to feed his family. It would be cooked in the day and smuggled into the cave at night, and by that time it would be spoiled and almost inedible. Yet it kept Thacienne and her family alive.

Within a week, things were beginning to settle down politically, and the process to change Rwanda from a monarchy to a republic moved quickly. Hutu leaders assumed control of the previously Tutsi-held positions over villages, towns, and cities, and the local governments declared peace and an end to the tumult in an effort to gain some control of the chaotic events that were happening across the nation. They gathered many of the Tutsis who were displaced from their homes and villages and in hiding, but those who had crossed the borders into neighbouring nations for fear of their lives were forbidden by the newly elected Hutu government to return.

News of peace came to the Mukaminega family and washed over them like cold water in a dry place. It had been a full week of eating rotten potatoes and beans and lying on a hard ground. But where to go still eluded them. Not only had their house been destroyed, their property had been seized. Anastase feared what would happen to his family if they even showed their faces around that area.

They arrived in nearby Ruhengeri City later that day, and they received limited shelter and nourishment from government aid. They would be driven with other Tutsi families 143 kilometres to Bugesera, a district in the Eastern Province of Rwanda.

Chapter 2
EXODUS

A RWANDAN LEGEND IS TOLD OF A DEITY NAMED KIGWA WHO HAD three sons, Gatutsi, Gahutu, and Gatwa. As he needed an heir, he tested his sons by giving them each a pot of milk to guard and watch over. Gatwa drank the milk, Gahutu fell asleep, and Gatutsi stayed awake, keeping guard over his milk. The result was that Gatutsi was chosen as Kigwa's successor, Gahutu was relegated as a servant to Gatutsi, and Gatwa became a foreigner and an outsider. It is said that this legend was fabricated by Tutsi elites to justify the social hierarchy during the Rwandan monarchy.

BEAUTIFUL RWANDA

Rwanda is beautiful. Between Tanzania and Burundi flows Kagera River, part of the upper headwaters of the Nile. From Lake Rweru in Burundi in the south it flows north alongside the Rwanda-Tanzania border and over Rusumo Falls, a historical landmark in Rwanda, forming a great ravine that doubles as a natural border between the two nations. Kagera River eventually works its way north to Uganda and eventually into the Nile. It was the scene of the first arrival of Europeans in Rwanda, Gustaf Von Gotzen of the Germans having crossed the famous river. Later in 1916 the Belgian victors of World War I crossed, after wrestling administration of the region from the Germans. But in 1994, these national landmarks that displayed the beauty of Rwanda to the developed world were a horror show.

By May of that year, halfway through the genocide, 10,000 bodies had been thrown down Rusumo Falls, causing health hazards in Uganda's fishing market downstream. Because water from almost every part of Rwanda drains into the Kagera River, bodies were carried from Rwanda into Lake Victoria in Uganda, where they caused a state of emergency. Carried by the current, they bobbled up and down in the river, clubbed, hacked, shot, burned, sometimes 100 corpses an hour. On one shore, 700 carcasses, bloated and mutilated, washed up. Some had their breasts and genitals sawed off, while the cadavers that were identified as pregnant women had their fetuses ripped out. Children were the hardest to look at. Apparently for efficiency, several children were pierced through with a spear, skewered like meat, and sent to the bottom of the falls.

Clean-up efforts in Uganda were hampered by the heavy African rains and wild scavengers drawn by the decomposing stench of the bodies that clung to the shores of the lake like seaweed in an ocean. To save the fishing economy, motorized boats were used to trap the bodies and bring them ashore. There another challenge presented itself, the safe handling and disposal of the carcasses. Those fishing in the poisoned water were warned to wash their catch thoroughly, and by the latter part of the genocide, fish hardly sold in those parts. By June, 40,000 bodies had floated down the falls.

THE CHAINING OF RWANDA'S SOUL

Before Von Gotzen had set foot on Rwanda's soil (then called Ruanda-Urundi, as Rwanda and Burundi were one nation), the Hutu majority citizens were ruled by Tutsi minority lords through an aristocracy. At the top of the hierarchy was the *mwami*, the Tutsi king, and then Tutsi chiefs were over the various provinces of Rwanda. While Hutus were, for the most part, an agricultural people and heavily relied on farming, Tutsis, who migrated to Rwanda centuries after the Hutus, came in with cattle, which they used to slowly establish a feudal class system, with the mwami being at the top. The Twas, a forest people who make up a single percentage of the Rwanda population, were the first to migrate to Rwanda. When Hutu people came into the land, Twas moved deeper into the forest.

The Hutu and Tutsi distinction was based more on class status, and it was not uncommon for Hutu and Tutsi statuses to be interchangeable based on cattle or another form of wealth. Anyone could also be Hutu if they were impoverished enough. However unjust and imperfect this system was, it maintained a form of structure and stability, and outbreaks of violence were foreign in those times.

At the Berlin Conference of 1884, Ruanda-Urundi was assigned as German East Africa, and von Gotzen, a German explorer, was appointed governor. Although a German colony, Ruanda-Urundi was loosely administrated, and the monarchy was allowed rulership. After World War I, Belgian forces took control of Ruanda-Urundi from their colony in Congo and received a mandate from the League of Nations to administrate Ruanda-Urundi. Once again, rulership was left to the Tutsi aristocracy, but as the Age of Eugenics raged on in Europe, it found itself in the hills of our small country.

At that time, Hutus and Tutsis were mostly peaceful, with little conflict. It was the Europeans who stressed eugenics and labelled Hutus and Tutsis as different races. As they continued to support and rule through the aristocracy led by the Tutsi mwami, they began to alienate Hutus by declaring Tutsi superiority as a genetic fact. Scientists arrived to measure skulls, equating them to brain size. The findings they published and distributed claimed that because Tutsis were taller, light-skinned and had larger skulls, they were superior to their Hutu counterparts. They came to believe that Tutsis had Caucasian features and therefore had Caucasian ancestry.

It was not long before identification cards were distributed and the Hutu-Tutsi divide was crystallized. Gone was the fluidity and class structure, now replaced by race and eugenics. All this continued while the Belgium colonizers subjected Hutus to manual labour and heaped praise and support on the Tutsis, encouraging, indeed mandating, a superiority complex. This would eventually backfire as seeds of genocide were planted.

Although Belgium occupation favoured the Tutsis, the idea of a free Rwanda, an independent nation, began to float among them. After World War II, Belgium received pressure for democratic reform from the international community, which was intensified by the then Rwandan king, who carried a strong democratic vision. The world was changing as a wave of decolonization was taking place. Between 1945 and 1960 alone, more than thirty states in Asia and Africa would be decolonized.

Meanwhile, the Hutu leaders sat back and watched, sensing an opportunity for a national restructuring. The identification cards that were supposed to distinguish and divide Hutus and Tutsis had also united Hutu people and solidified the notion that, although they were an opposition party, they were by far the majority in the land. The Belgians perceived a coming shift and, also seeing an economic advantage post-independence, slowly began to support the rising Hutu public.

In 1957, nine Hutu intellectuals led by Gregoire Kayibanda penned the "Bahutu Manifesto," a political document that called for Hutu dominance and freedom from the "Belgium occupiers" and their "Tutsi puppets." Between 1957 and 1959 there were a series of controversies and assassinations attempts, which finally reached the boiling point when a Hutu politician named Dominique Mbanyumutwa was taken and beaten by Tutsi activists. What followed was the "Wind of Destruction," Rwanda's revolution war, which almost overnight reversed the ruling structure from Tutsis to Hutus, all while Belgian forces continued to quietly support the Hutu revolutionists.

In the ensuing aftermath, nearly 100,000 Tutsis were killed, and one-third of the Tutsi population had fled and were living in exile throughout bordering nations, in Zaire (now the Democratic Republic of Congo), Tanzania, and Uganda. Across Ruanda-Urundi, Tutsi chiefs were assassinated, and those who remained were excluded from power. The same rhetoric that the European colonists had brought in, claiming that Tutsis and Hutus were of different races, was adopted by the Hutu leadership and used to discredit Tutsis. If they were indeed from Caucasian ancestry, then they were also aliens and foreigners to Rwanda. Rather than reject the baseless research of eugenic scientists, they embraced the myths as fact and fed it to their people as justification for the decades of propaganda against Tutsis that would follow.

In 1962, the now openly pro-Hutu Belgian administration held elections, and the nation voted to overthrow the monarchy. Ruanda-Urundi became Rwanda and Burundi, and Rwanda became a republic. It was in this madness that young Thacienne found herself.

A PLACE CALLED HELL

It was hard to miss the sea of white United Nations tents scattered across the Nyamata area, the accommodation for thousands of displaced Tutsis, now refugees in their homeland. The smell of human waste and body odour blended with the humidity and welcomed many more Tutsis arriving in trucks.

There was nothing good about this place. Nyamata's water was swampy and infested with crocodiles. But much worse was the fact that there were hardly any latrines, if any, which contributed to the various diseases that plagued this place. Thacienne heard the scream of a woman who had doubtlessly lost a child, as she called out his name between sobs. Thacienne recalled seeing sick children being taken to the infirmary who never returned. Whether from malaria or typhoid, people died on a regular basis. Although the United Nations (UN) supplied rations to the thousands of refugees, the food was foreign to their diet and only resulted into more maladies. Weeping and despair were heard all through the night, and in the morning, another person would be missing and presumed dead.

UN volunteers busily attended to the people, handing out rations and supplies. Truckloads of refugees from all across Rwanda were being deposited like a garbage truck unloads its contents at a city dump. Years later, Thacienne would remark that she understood how the Jews felt as they were being driven to concentration camps but thought they were being taken to new settlements. *Nyamata* means "place of milk" in Rwandese, but this place was not a resettlement opportunity for the displaced Tutsis; it was a death camp.

HEAVEN'S WHISPER

Thacienne's skin was light-toned, and her gentle voice matched her innocent personality. In fact, I see her often in your strength, London, and in your smile, Kyleigh. In her small village in Musanze, her laugh preceded her presence, and her smile seemed permanent. But living in this place began to change her. Fear and hopelessness hung over her like a dark cloud, and, seeing the carnage and hopelessness of that land, she began to retreat into herself. She had never seen or experienced such suffering. No amount of washing could remove the stench of death that seemed to cling to her, and no amount of screaming could drown out the desperate cries of malnourished infants and newly made orphans. People regularly died from dehydration and malnutrition if the diseases did not get them. She began to see the frailty of life and to wonder if there was anything she could do to beat against the dread. Even at her young age Thacienne understood that unless there was an intervention, her family would become another statistic in the growing death rates of the Nyamata refugee camp.

As she lay on the hard ground one particular night, that feeling of hopelessness accompanied the deep darkness that enveloped her. Then something within her began to stir. She found her mind wandering to thoughts of eternity as if someone from that realm was drawing her, calling out to her.

Thacienne got up, gingerly planted her knees on the hard ground, and whispered the only prayer she could think of. "Dear God, please send Your guardian angel to watch over me." At that moment, it was as if hope was personified, for it descended on her like a warm blanket and covered her. God answered her simple prayer, and for more evenings to come, Thacienne prayed the same prayer and saw the same results. No life-threatening sickness or disease afflicted her or anyone else in her family. That pivotal moment forever shaped her life, for she discovered a loving Father who smiled upon her in the midst of the forsaken refugee masses of Nyamata.

REBELS WITH CAUSE

In 1964, the Congo Crisis that saw 100,000 people killed and resulted in its liberation from Belgium colonists was in full swing. Congo sat hugging the southwest corner of Rwanda and had been a haven for the Tutsis who had escaped the revolution. Taking advantage of their disorientation, factions in their host nation recruited them to secure Congo's independence, something they succeeded at.

After the Congo Crisis, the emboldened Rwandan refugees, still seething over their banishment half a decade before, decided to mount a war against the Hutu Rwandan government. They invaded Rwanda from Congo in the west as well as from Burundi to the south. After handily defeating an army outpost close to Nyamata, the Tutsi rebels arrived into Nyamata itself and witnessed the conditions that their people were in. Angered at the treatment of their countrymen, the rebels began a campaign to recruit the disillusioned men in Nyamata who had no cause.

By this time, Nyamata's residents had found that their internment residence was not as bad as they had previously thought. The land turned out to be fertile, and there was rain in season. Eventually there were some good harvests, and people began to live, not just survive. Anastase had managed to secure a small piece of land outside Nyamata and built a modest home and farm where they could be away from the overpopulated camp and safe from the marauding Hutu armies that frequented the area.

Knowing that the refugees' planned attempt at an attack against Kigali would result in more trouble and a greater military presence in Nyamata, Anastase forbade his boys from taking part in it. However, many men rallied around their kin from Congo and gathered whatever makeshift weapons they could find, elated to play a part in unseating the Hutu regime that had driven them away. Then hundreds of men began their seventy-kilometre march to the capital city.

The much better armed and trained Hutu army met them on the way. The Tutsi patriots were handily defeated and were scattered across the countryside, and many returned to their homes and families in shame. Meanwhile, the Hutu army traced the source of the rebellion to Bugesera district, where Nyamata is. A few days later, a military convoy rolled into the district and rounded up as many men as they could find. They brought them to Nyamata, in the centre of the refugee camp, which had now been converted into a village, and systematically slaughtered every male before the eyes of their petrified wives and children.

A few days later, another military convoy repeated the massacre, murdering as many men as they could gather. Some bodies were thrown in the river close by. Others they left to rot under the heavy rays of the sun, a reminder of what would happen to rebels. Fear gripped every family, not knowing when a convoy would arrive for the next slaughter.

Not too far removed from Nyamata, the Mukaminega family had been celebrating. Euphrasie was the oldest daughter, and her fun-loving and carefree personality had won over the affection of a certain young man in Nyamata. Anastase and Bernadette, as well as all of the family, had watched as the two of them spoke wedding vows over one another and strolled away to their new home for their honeymoon. For a while, the horrors of war and death were forgotten, especially when Euphrasie excitedly announced to her family and neighbours that she was pregnant.

Euphrasie never would have thought that her husband, his brothers, and his father would be in Nyamata the day the convoy rolled through. She never would have thought they would be taken along with the other men to the centre of the village. She never would have thought they would be shot and killed, their bodies lying lifeless among a gory pile. She never would have thought that she would be a widow and her child would grow up never knowing a father.

Not long after the death of Euphrasie's husband, Thacienne prepared some food to take to her grieving sister, who was getting closer and closer to delivery. She took her time strolling down the road and stopped to pick up flowers and watch birds singing high in the trees. Then she detected a rank smell that had become familiar to her. Tinged with a little bit of sweetness, the smell grew more pungent and nauseating as she continued down the road. It was like rotting meat dabbed with cheap perfume.

Thacienne cupped her nose and tried to block the pungent stench, but as she walked on it was suddenly all around her. In fear, Thacienne started to run to evade the reek, just as her eyes caught the source lying in the ditch a few feet from her. He was now bloated and discoloured, eyes bulging out and a swollen tongue protruding from his mouth as heaps of maggots climbed over each other, invading every crevice. It was one of the young men who lived close to the village and had fallen prey to the convoy.

Even for a ten-year-old, this had become the new normal. But for all that was taking a place around her, the idea that a divine hand had protected her and her family through plague and ploy had already established itself. Even in the midst of extreme suffering, a hope remained.

AN UNLIKELY ADVOCATE

Things began to settle down, and the Rwandan army backed off on the killing. Instead, they set up a permanent post in Nyamata and designated civilians around the village to keep watch over the people and report back, lest another revolt take place. Accusations brought up against Nyamata's inhabitants would warrant immediate execution. False allegations abounded, and an unwillingness to investigate those accusations meant the deaths of more and more Tutsi men.

It was at this time that an envoy came to the Mukaminega household, inviting Anastase to report to the middle of the village. He had been accused. The realization that they might never see their father again sent fear into the Mukaminegas. There was no caves to hide in and no way of escape to another region. If any event could bring down the Mukaminega family, it was the loss of their patriarch. The false witness that had accused him would be waiting for him, and there was no chance of Anastase finding a friend among the Hutu condemners, save divine assistance.

Anastase slowly made his way to the centre of the village. As he drew near he could see the dead bodies of other men who had received the same invitation. His name was called, and he stood before the tribunal. Accusations were made of conspiracy against the government. But in the midst of the false witnesses, one voice of support emerged from the masses of people who watched.

Anastase turned to face a Hutu man he did not know yet seemed to know him. The man vouched for him and declared that Anastase was innocent and should be pardoned of any wrongdoings charged against him. To the amazement of those watching, Anastase was cleared of all accusations and was released to return to his family.

JOURNEY IN THE DARK

A Rwandan proverb says, "There is not a place where peace reigns at night," meaning that peace is nowhere. In a country that was being ravaged by prejudice and swallowed up in a never-ending conflict, it seemed like there was nowhere to hide. For many days, Anastase sat in silence, nothing being heard but the puff of his pipe, contemplating their next move. His narrow brush with death was all the reason he needed to flee. He feared for his family and what would become of them if they remained in a country that grew increasingly hostile.

After much thought, the only option he could find was to leave the country entirely. Burundi sat to the south of Rwanda and was the ideal location. But Anastase understood that this was not just his decision to make, and Bernadette would need strong convincing to make the daring escape from relative security into the complete unknown.

Many other families had been desperate enough to risk their lives in the vast and densely wooded area filled with wild animals. Because of the patrols by the military during the day, they had to travel under cover of darkness, choosing to face the wild beasts of the night rather than the machetes and rifles of the day. Some had made it, but many had fallen prey along the way, and this is what concerned Bernadette above all else. Sure, many had successfully ventured into the forest and arrived in the relatively safe neighbouring country, but those were men travelling in pairs and at times by themselves. Those who made the journey with women and children often didn't make it. She understood the need to flee and begin life anew, but the stinging feeling that they would not survive the journey continued to nip at her.

Anastase and Bernadette came to a compromise. Jean-Baptiste, the eldest of the Mukaminega children, would be sent first to scout the layout of the land, so-to-speak, and would return with a report. Based on that, they would decide whether or not they would risk the journey.

The news Jean-Baptiste brought back was enough to convince Bernadette that it was worth it. Busoni, in the Burundi province of Kirundo, sat a few miles from the Rwanda-Burundi border. It was a hilly, moist land with a very close water source. The UN was also on site, taking care of those who had made the journey from Rwanda, and there were many local farmers whom Anastase could form a partnership with to provide for his family. No burning heat, no mosquitoes and black flies—this was Canaan to Nyamata's Egypt! The only downside was that Busoni was sixty kilometres away from Nyamata with thick jungles standing in the way. Travelling there only at night and treading carefully to avoid the detection of wild beasts, all with women and children, would take days.

With 120,000 Tutsi people living outside of Rwanda because of fear of the Hutu government, it was not unusual to see travelling caravans of people attempting to cross the wild forests into neighbouring Burundi. What was unusual was those who would make it. Government soldiers roamed the area looking for families and individuals leaving the country. Whoever was caught would be accused of having the intent of joining the rebel forces that continued to train in hopes of returning to Rwanda, and they were usually executed. But in the minds of many Tutsis, their only choice was either a swift execution if they were caught or a slow death if they remained. So the Mukaminega family made preparations, connected with other families that planned to escape, and waited for the proper time.

It was nighttime when Thacienne's third exodus began. Under cover of darkness, the group eluded the flashlights in the distance of roaming patrols and dived into the thick midst of that African forest. The chirping of crickets and the croaking of frogs filled the jungle, but it was not what they could hear that bothered them; it was what they couldn't. Who could know if the hidden carnivores that stalked their prey in the night were watching? The group surmised that as long as they remained close together they would seem a threat to watching predators.

At times they would approach homes that belonged to the natives of that land, but they steered clear in case the inhabitants deemed them a threat and drew the attention of the authorities. When the sun rose in the mornings, they would settle in a well-hidden area and take turns sleeping and resting while others stood sentry. But as the sun went down and the jungle life came to life with the chorus of chirping and croaking, the small band of refugees continued their careful journey to freedom. After three days, they crossed the border into Burundi and sang for joy.

Chapter 3
A NEW BEGINNING

A NATION APART

AS THACIENNE'S FAMILY SETTLED IN BURUNDI, RWANDA CONTINUED TO be torn apart. In 1961, there was a referendum on whether the monarchy should remain or be abolished. The nation overwhelmingly voted to disband the monarchy, and after an election, the MDR-Parmehutu (Party for the Hutu Emancipation) party won thirty-five of the forty-four electoral seats, ushering Rwanda into independence in 1962. Gregoire Kayibanda, Parmehutu's founder, was elected as president shortly after independence, and by 1965 Parmehutu was Rwanda's only legal party.

Kayibanda was not a good man. He was born in a place in Rwanda called Tare, and in 1957 he, along with eight Hutu intellectuals, wrote the "Hutu Manifesto," a political ideology calling for liberation from the Belgian colonists and political exile for the Tutsi people, whom they called "oppressors." Kayibanda used the word *inyenzi*, Rwandese for "cockroach," in reference to Tutsis. With the overwhelming political power now in Hutu hands, disorganized violence against Tutsis was carried out across the country, with Parmehutu doing little to quench it. Kayibanda meanwhile executed moderate Hutu figures and got rid of oppositional Tutsi parties, making Parmehutu the only legitimate political party in Rwanda.

Fearing for their lives and the possibility of another "Wind of Destruction," thousands of Tutsis began fleeing the country. By 1964, over 150,000 Tutsis had become refugees in foreign lands. Burundi, being a Tutsi-run country, was flooded with tens of thousands of refugees and became a hotbed for Tutsi militia intent on regaining control in Rwanda. The 1960s were marked with attempt after attempt of failed campaigns against the Hutu government of Rwanda from said militia groups. With each Tutsi failure and Parmehutu victory, hostility was renewed and violence was carried out against the remaining Tutsis in Rwanda in order to punish them for what their kin were doing across the borders.

As Rwanda continued to be dragged through the mud in the '60s, Parmehutu began pushing the propaganda that the difference between Tutsi and Hutu people was that of race and not ethnicity. If this was the case, then Tutsis were alien and non-indigenous—not truly Rwandan nationals. This train of thought was touted in official literature and taught in schools and universities across the country, further dividing the fragile nation. Not only had Tutsi involvement disappeared in government, but their enrolment in education had dwindled. This new teaching had relegated the Tutsi people as second class citizens in their own homeland.

As Kayibanda continued to inflict his cruel, dictatorial policies, Rwanda suffered both economically and diplomatically.

A new policy established by the Parmehutu government was the enforcement of ethnic quotas in education and public sector jobs, with the Hutu people receiving a vast share of them. Rwanda, particularly Kayibanda, had earned a negative international reputation and was paying a heavy price for it.

Kayibanda's cousin and defence minister, Major General Juvénal Habyarimana, then seized power by ousting Parmehutu and overthrowing Gregoire Kayibanda. Although it was considered a bloodless coup, many high ranking Parmehutu officials were reportedly executed. It is said that Kayibanda was placed under house arrest, where he eventually died. He had held office for twelve years.

Habyarimana entered office as Rwanda's second president, promising domestic stability and a rollback of the hardline policies instituted by his predecessor. The Hutu and Tutsi difference was officially changed from "racial" to "ethnic," he sought to balance the ethnic quota in the educational field and the public sector, and he also lifted the moratorium of Tutsis in government. Yet for all of his efforts, nothing could change what had been brewing for decades.

PROMISED LAND

As things in Rwanda sped towards disaster, life in Burundi seemed to slow down for Thacienne. She had found a new home far removed from the chaos she was used to. Life was not perfect though, especially for a refugee family in a foreign land. Anastase would need to work twice as hard to get what native Burundians received. But what was there to complain about? They had found peace and refuge without losing a single member of the family. As far as they were concerned, this was their Promised Land.

As years passed and Thacienne's older siblings left home in search of spouses and careers, Anastase and Bernadette looked east to neighbouring Tanzania. Following Nyerere's presidency, Tanzania had become a socialist country, and with many large industries nationalized, it would be easier to find work and property there. By this time, Thacienne was preparing to enter college in hopes of being a teacher. Tanzania seemed safe, and the idea of her parents leaving her in Burundi alone was unnerving, yet she remained committed to her dream. Knowing that she was out of place and that odds were stacked against her as a refugee only strengthened her resolve to succeed. Her parents were poor, she had no backup plans if she failed school, and she had no prospects of marriage. All she had was a distant memory. She remembered the thick air, the stench of disease, and the bleak darkness. But she also remembered a whisper, the prayer she had prayed many years before: "Dear God, please send Your guardian angel to watch over me." She clung to the One who had answered her that night and for many nights after. The One who had seen her through the perilous journey in the night to Burundi would get her into college. And He did.

A WALK WITH GOD

With her parents far away and no one she knew close by, it did not take long for Thacienne to read the writing on the wall: there was no turning back. College was nothing like high school. Gone were petty rivalries, silly gossip, and nonsensical crushes. Her teachers were tough, and the competition was fierce.

Started by missionaries with the purpose of aiding the poor, the teacher training college that Thacienne, now seventeen years of age, attended would the starting point for the rest of her life.

Although the teachers demanded discipline and hard work, something else dominated the campuses and flowed through the faculties. It was a gentle peace that Thacienne had never known but desperately wanted to experience. One teacher in particular was an elderly woman from Ireland who had fallen in love with Africa. Thacienne was immediately attracted to her devotion to God and would repeatedly visited her in the library to hear her read books and tell stories.

Thacienne had discovered God in the darkness of the Nyamata night, but she lacked knowledge of what other steps to take in her walk with God. So when travelling preachers and missionaries visited the school, she would savour each message and testimony. She spent hours in the library reading and studying the Bible, and Watchman Nee and Brother Andrew became her guides into knowledge of the kingdom of God, their great classic literature being her companions. Her prayers to God throughout her teenage life, although somewhat effective, had been repetitive and shallow. She now joined a college prayer group of mostly older students and faculty members, wanting to learn how to pray with power and boldness. She hungered to see miracles like she read about in books and heard about from missionaries out on the fields.

The Irish teacher introduced Thacienne to Corrie ten Boom's *Tramp for the Lord*. As she read about the woman who loved the Gestapo officers and Nazi soldiers who mistreated her during the Holocaust, it was inconceivable to her that Corrie could choose to forgive her enemies. Thacienne wondered if she could have the courage to forgive as Corrie had done. But it was while reading about Yona Kanamuzeyi that she met Jesus.

Being Tutsi, Yona Kanamuzeyi and his family had been taken to the same refugee camp as Thacienne in Nyamata, but they never met. Yona felt that God had him there for a reason, and he took the opportunity to show the love of Jesus to the residents of that filthy land. When Tutsi refugees from Burundi attacked Kigali, many Rwandans fled to Burundi, including the Mukaminega family, but Yona chose to remain in Nyamata, encouraging the people and teaching them about the kingdom of God. On January 23, 1964, Yona read Psalm 27:3-4:

Though an army encamp against me, my heart shall not fear; though war rise against me, yet I will be confident. One thing have I asked of the LORD, that will I seek after: that I may dwell in the house of the LORD all the days of my life, to gaze upon the beauty of the LORD and to inquire in his temple.

That evening, six soldiers showed up at his home and arrested him. They took him to Nyaborongo with two more prisoners, and after he prayed that God would forgive his captors, their hands were bound. But something peculiar happened in that moment; a song burst from the prisoners, including Yona, as they sang the old hymn "There Is a Happy Land Far, Far Away." The annoyed soldiers grabbed Yona, shot him, and threw his body into the river. But even as he died, the song continued to flow from his lips, cutting to the very core of the stunned soldiers. Not knowing what to do next, for they had never seen anyone die singing, they released the other two prisoners.

As Thacienne read this account, tears welled up. She calmly put the book aside and made a commitment to the invisible God who had been present with her all along. She would never waver from Him, she would not marry someone who did not love Him, and, she decided, her life was now His. (I'm anticipating the day when you will make that decision, London and Kyleigh.)

SEASON OF MIRACLES

The world became different for Thacienne. A foreign love welled up for her peers who knew God, and mercy flowed from her to those who did not, although she yearned for them to be acquainted with the One she now knew. She clearly saw how God had been at work in her family, protecting and guiding them through the turmoil of war and fear. It was not His absence that caused them to flee from their homes with barely their lives—it was His mercy. Grace provided the caves that became their home, and by His providence they were fed. Even in the heat and plague of Nyamata they left unscathed under His watchful eye.

(And this I want you to understand, London and Kyleigh: it is often easy to view challenges in a pessimistic way and conclude that God is far away. But oftentimes it is the opposite, for when we see with optimistic eyes we realize that He was as close as ever. For had it not been for Him, something far worse might have occurred. Two things became clear in your fight to survive as "extreme preemies": that there is a real evil force of darkness that sought your destruction, and that that force pales in comparison to the overwhelming grace of God, which responded and caused you to live. It's all in how you see it, whether pessimistically or optimistically.)

In the kingdom above the clouds, the king smiled, and heaven celebrated. It is written that there is great rejoicing when one person is made a citizen (Luke 15:7). The Thacienne who froze in terror at the sight of her home lit up in flames, before caves became her dwelling place, was transformed. The Bible says that if we take the first step and draw near to God, He will draw near to us (James 4:8), as a Father to a child. The season that followed Thacienne's dedication to a Heavenly Father became a season of heaven's presence drawing nearer and nearer. "If God is truly my Father," she reasoned, "then He will take care of the needs that I have." And she had many.

Compared to other girls in the college, Thacienne's closet was depressing. Apart from her school uniform, she only had a couple of dresses to wear. At one point, she only had one dress to wear on a Sunday, and she had lent it to a friend over the week. As the weekend loomed closer, she had nothing but a school uniform to wear to church. Her earthly parents were miles away in Tanzania and were unable to offer assistance, but she remembered that she had a Heavenly Father, so she cried out to Him to supply a dress.

When Sunday morning came, she sat in her bedroom wearing her uniform, watching the other girls walk past her in their weekend best. Then it happened. Just as she was about to leave for the service in her school uniform, a friend of hers, who was completely oblivious to her need, ran into her room looking for her. Coming from a wealthier home, she had many dresses and wanted Thacienne to pick any one she wanted! Though it seems small, to Thacienne it was as big as God. It was not the fact that she received a dress to wear—that was indeed small. What was big was that Thacienne had asked, and the God of the universe had answered.

At another point, it was in the middle of the school year, and Thacienne only had fifty francs to her name. One day, a man stopped at the school, desperately seeking monetary assistance. Some students gave to the need, including Thacienne, who gave her remaining fifty francs, trusting that the God who dressed her would also repay the funds she had given in goodwill. It was not long before a couple who lived in the neighbourhood and knew about Thacienne being far from home brought an envelope to her. It had fifty francs in it.

Thacienne also noticed that her love for people, including those who stood against her as enemies, was growing. As refugees, Rwandans in the predominant Burundian school had to work extra hard to make it. Such was the nature of survival in a foreign land, and they accepted it. But some Burundians saw that the Rwandans were getting better marks in class, and jealousy ensued. As a result, many refugees were isolated and viciously mocked, including Thacienne. Brimming with joy because of her new-found life, Thacienne refused to retaliate as many of her peers did and instead was kind and friendly to her Burundian friends, Yona Kanamuzeyi's and Corrie ten Boom's stories afresh in her mind.

Unknown to Thacienne, God was preparing her for the greatest act of forgiveness she would ever have to face.

Chapter 4
LOVE STORY

THE TIME WAS 11:45 A.M., FIFTEEN MINUTES BEFORE LUNCH BREAK, AND lunch could not come fast enough. The mornings seemed to go by the slowest, and very soon his stomach would be vocal, alerting everyone in close proximity that Alphonse Karuhije was hungry. It was not that he disliked school; he genuinely enjoyed it, counting it as an honour for a poor fatherless Tutsi boy to receive an education in a Hutu-ruled world. Not even the federally fixed quotas limiting the number of Tutsis participating in Rwanda's education system could have barred him from stepping into the call that God had for him. Ishogwe was the name of the school.

He had read in the Bible that God would go before him to make the crooked paths straight, smash through the gates of bronze, and cut through the iron bars, so Alphonse was not foolish enough to take any credit for his good fortune in receiving education. His father had fallen into deep waters and drowned when Alphonse was a young boy, the very time he needed him the most. His mother had remarried her late husband's brother for economic stability, and Alphonse's cousins became his siblings. He had fallen prey to the anti-Tutsi bullying and hazing everywhere he went, and it bothered him to no end, until he had made a life-changing discovery.

Ishogwe School sat beside an all-girls school that had gone through a revival. As a result, many girls came to Ishogwe to evangelize the students, and God took the opportunity to grab hold of Alphonse's heart in a powerful way. As many of his peers gushed over the looks of the friendly members of the fairer sex, Alphonse was taken back by their genuine joy and peace, which was foreign in his world. For the first time, Alphonse realized that he was not an orphan. Beyond the clouds sat a vast kingdom, and the King was his Father. When he made the decision to follow Him, Alphonse knew he was destined for adventures in greatness. Now, if he could just get through this class and replenish his belly...

As the teacher drew the lesson to a close, Alphonse began to gather his books, anticipating dismissal. *Pop!* It sounded like thunder, but it wasn't. *Pop! Pop!* The sound of gunshots was impossible to mistake; Tutsis knew it well. Alphonse's peers, who moments ago had sat bored, went berserk. Screaming and scattering, his classmates ran outside, tripping and stepping over one another and running for any shelter they could find. Alphonse was right with them, shouting to friends of his who were searching for a place to hide. They took off for the nearby woods and did not look back as gunshots exploded around them and students screamed, some dropping to the ground, lifeless. Panic overtook Alphonse as his legs turned to jelly, but he pushed himself to press on. One misstep or pause, and a bullet would find him or, worse, he could be caught.

He knew the drill, as did almost every Tutsi. There was no use going back and fighting. Standing up to the murderers who now rampaged through the school in search of inyenzi would be standing up to the entire Rwandan government.

Alphonse and his friends continued to run, and they would not stop until it was physically impossible. Gunshots and screams grew fainter and fainter behind him, but he continued to run, his stomach growling.

HIS NAME IS PASTOR

"What kind of name is *Pastor*?" Thacienne was not sure if it was his actual name or his occupation.

"I don't know! That is the only name I've heard them use for him."

It was the summer of 1975. Years had passed since Thacienne's time in college, and she had found a job teaching grades 1 and 3 in a missionary-run Methodist school. With her school days behind her, her faith in Jesus had strengthened, grounded in the foundation of Bible studies and prayer meetings. She found herself wanting more of God's Word, never satisfied enough to stop learning and growing.

Towards the close of her time at the teacher training school, her favourite thing was hearing the guest speakers and missionaries who would pass through. Her mind would race with thoughts of preaching and teaching God's Word, seeing miracles performed, and leading many into a relationship like the one she now enjoyed with her Heavenly Father. It was not long before her dreams would be fulfilled.

She joined an on-campus prayer meeting group called "Abarokore" (Rwandese for "Redeemed"), made up of about fifteen girls who were zealous for God's work. They would go into different churches in the community, where they would be welcomed to preach and teach God's Word. It was as if she was living what she had only read about in books as people were healed at the touch of a hand, many were converted, and other believers' faith was encouraged as they saw young people who were passionate for the things of God.

Graduation had come and gone, and after finding a job as a teacher, she had settled down to focus on her career, but a fire for the gospel remained in her heart. Almost everyone who knew Thacienne Mukaminega saw her depth and passion for the God who had saved her multiple times. Many suitors came knocking on her door, but they were turned back if they did not have an authentic and genuine heart to know her Saviour. Her promise to Him that she would not wed anyone who was not committed to Him was fresh on her mind. This was part of the reason she was having this conversation with her friend in the first place.

It was summer, and being a teacher, she had the opportunity to rest and refresh. Her friend had invited her to Bujumbura, Burundi's capital city, for a few weeks, and they were staying in her brother's home. Her friend was now telling her about this man they called "Pastor," which was odd because he was not a pastor. His real name was Alphonse Karuhije, and she would be meeting him that night.

The visit could not have been more perfect. Alphonse was a gentleman and loved God intensely. She now understood why all his friends had dubbed him *Pastor*. Despite all that he had been through and the hardships he had endured, his faith in God was unshakable. They talked about their families, their respective escapes to Burundi, and their current occupations, but more than anything they talked about God. After years of wondering if she would meet someone who shared her affections, was it possible that she had?

To Alphonse, it was not just possible; it was sealed! After visiting with her a few more times that summer, he was convinced that Thacienne was the one for him. Long after the summer ended and Thacienne returned to her small town to teach, Alphonse continued to write to her, candid about the way he felt about her. But as weeks turned to months, the year grew longer, and the busyness of school kicked in, Thacienne began to forget the connection she shared with Alphonse and how she had felt while talking to him for hours on end. She by no means forgot the person Alphonse—his letters made sure of that—but after a time he seemed far away, as did the possibility that they would end up together. Besides, another option had presented itself.

PIO

Pio was a native Burundian and a teacher. Through a mutual friend, he had met Thacienne, and being smitten by her, he did not waste any time pursuing her. Thacienne was not convinced that he was "the one," but as time passed and her friends encouraged her, she found herself giving in to his advances. He was handsome and educated, and he was even a Christian, so what was there not to like? Yet it seemed to her that something was not right. Meanwhile, Alphonse's letters kept streaming in.

At the behest of her friends, Thacienne agreed to marry Pio, and wedding planning began. Her family was excited, her friends were excited, but something continued to trouble Thacienne.

She observed the way he treated his friends and family and how he was to her, and slowly she realized that she was making a mistake. Having already committed to him and having told her family, she did not want the drama and stigmatization that would come from breaking off an engagement, yet she knew she could not possibly go through with it. Unsure of what to do, Thacienne found herself on her knees again in prayer, just as she had been as a little girl in Nyamata. And the more she prayed, the more she realized that their relationship was not right.

As time passed and the wedding date drew nearer, she made the decision that she would not pursue it. The dilemma was how to tell him that she was calling off the wedding with no evident reason except for the voice of her conscience.

DISASTER AVERTED

Thacienne chose her quiet time between the end of her classes and dinner to pray for the relationship, that God would end it and do it swiftly. Meanwhile, the letters kept coming in from Alphonse, who had not quit on her, but the baboon and gazelle Burundian stamps had been replaced by England's Queen Elizabeth II in royal blue; Alphonse had been accepted into a Bible school in Bristol, England. Thacienne marvelled at the favour of God that followed this man. A fatherless Tutsi refugee of Rwanda in a foreign land with no connections had been selected to be flown to England to attend a seminary? He had sensed God's confirmation that he was to be working in ministry full time and had embraced and cherished that call. Wanting to further his education in preparation for the work of God before him, he sent a letter to All Nations College in England, asking if he would be considered for seminary, and not only had he been approved; someone had paid his tuition in full! Something like this was unheard of, yet there he was—it was a true testimony of God working in his life.

Alphonse had learned of Thacienne's engagement to Pio, whom he also knew, but he held hope in his heart that she would be his. Not long before his departure, divine fortune had found them at the same youth conference, and Thacienne had remembered why this man was so special. She felt herself being pulled to him again as they spoke with excitement and passion about God's Word. She had forgotten how hours would breeze by when they spent time together and how alive she felt after their conversations. Towards the end of the conference, they went for a walk together, and that was when Alphonse gave her the news of the enormous opportunity he had just received abroad. Thacienne was genuinely happy for him, but she also knew what this meant. Gone would be the summer walks in Bujumbura, the long talks through the night, and the companionship of a man she had grown to admire. But it seemed that God had other plans, and who was she to stand in the way? Alphonse excitedly explained how he would need to commit to learning the English language and grasping the European culture. She began to congratulate him, but he was not finished speaking yet. "Thacienne," he said, "marry me."

As much as Thacienne had come to cherish their friendship and mutual love for God and His Word, this could not happen. She was already engaged to Pio and could not see herself breaking it off. This was before she began to have doubts about Pio, and at that point things were going well, and she was used to the idea of being married to him. Besides, Alphonse was starting a whole new life abroad, and she could not see herself there—

it was impossible. Thacienne politely declined and jokingly said that if things did not work out with Pio, three other men were lined up to court her. The ever-persistent Alphonse looked at her and politely asked if he could be the fourth.

He had flown to England, and that was that, except he was still writing to her, convinced that they were meant to be together. As her relationship with Pio looked more and more uncertain, she found her thoughts drifting back to Alphonse.

Shortly after, Pio returned from a conference on Bujumbura and asked to speak to Thacienne. He told her that he had heard God speak to him while he was at the conference and that he was not to marry her. Thacienne could hardly believe it. Could this be true? She looked up to heaven, to the Father who had once again come to her rescue, and began to thank Him for what He had just averted.

With that relationship behind her, she renewed her promise not to marry anyone who did not share her passion for Jesus and her love for the Word of God. Yet as news reached her family and peers that her engagement to Pio had been called off, rumours of her unfaithfulness and his rejection abounded. Although it did not bother her at first, as days and weeks rolled on she found herself doubting the whole chain of events. Had God really stepped in, or did Pio see something that was wrong with her? He had not given her a satisfying reason why he was breaking off the engagement. Was there something in fact wrong with her? As she caught wind of what was being spoken about her, she felt the sting of shame and disgrace.

One day as she watched her students playing outside, she began to reflect on the fact that she was alone and possibly unwanted by would be suitors. Hot tears rushed to her eyes at the wrongful accusations that were levelled against her and her inability to justify herself. Not wanting the children to see her, she rushed to find a room to cry in peace. She finally found a private room, and as she reached for the doorknob, she heard the Voice. It was audible to her, clear as day. Her hand froze on the doorknob. The Voice she had yearned to hear since she read stories of Abraham and Moses in the Old Testament was now speaking to her. It was strong and authoritative, yet gentle and pulsating with love, but there was no doubting that this was the God of the universe. "I will wipe the tears from your eyes." Immediately her tears dried up, and no more were shed over this situation. Her Father was with her.

A HEAVENLY DREAM

In addition to not marry anyone who was not a Christian, Thacienne made a commitment not to marry anyone at all until she knew that she *knew* that he was the one for her. It wouldn't be long. As she slept one evening, she had a dream of a jumbo airplane flying over her home and dropping letters as it flew by. She watched in her dream as people ran out to the pile of letters that now lay on the ground. A friend emerged from the pile, calling for her and holding a letter from England and claiming that her fiancé was writing to her. Thacienne immediately woke up.

She lived with two friends, also teachers at the same school, and as she sat down for breakfast that morning, the same friend who had brought the letter in her dream came in carrying a letter for her. Thacienne marvelled as her dream played out in front of her, and clutching the letter she read the name of the sender: Alphonse Karuhije. Her fiancé was writing to her.

As Alphonse's first year of school came to a close, he wrote to Thacienne, asking her to marry him. She gladly accepted. Sensing that God leading Alphonse to stay in Europe, they began to pray for God to make a way for her to be in England. Once again, God answered with a miracle, prompting a couple from Alphonse's church to pay for her travel and stay in England.

As the latest chapter in her life was coming to a close, all Thacienne could do was marvel at the goodness of the person she had come to know and experience as Father. She recalled the troubles of war, the poverty of being a refugee in a foreign land, and the departure of her family to another country, leaving her alone. Yet she was not alone. Through every situation, Heaven had answered mightily and resoundingly, capping it with God's personal promise that He would wipe every tear from her eyes. As she boarded the plane to the next stage in her adventure of faith, she realized that she never would have thought that a poor Tutsi refugee from Rwanda would ever travel to England. The giant Boeing 777, the first one she had been close to, seemed big to her. But her God had proved Himself bigger.

Chapter 5
THE CHAINING OF RWANDA'S SOUL

I ONCE READ AN ARTICLE ABOUT THE PSYCHOLOGY OF ABUSE PERPEtrators and victims. One story described a woman named Maria who had suffered years of verbal and physical abuse at the hands of her husband. It started small but quickly escalated. Yet for all the danger she was in, she faithfully returned to him, hoping he would change. It took a head contusion, from her husband slamming her head into their porcelain sink so hard that it broke in pieces, for her to permanently leave him. She was hospitalized, and her husband was sent to jail.

It was hard to understand why she would succumb to him and his violence for all that time. Surely she could have reported him or at the very least left him, but she resigned herself to the constant beating and shaming. She even rationalized that somehow she was to blame for his ruffian ways. He would tell her that she was no good and that even a simple thing like washing dishes was beyond her. Those words ate at her self-worth, and she accused herself of not being good enough for him. Accepting his volatile habits as her fault, she believed that any evil she received was just and perhaps even well-deserved.

Self-blame amplifies our inadequacies, whether real or imagined, and paralyzes us. Living in fear, embarrassment, and self-blame, victims of domestic violence may try to escape but feel isolated and insecure, too ashamed to tell their loved ones. In many cases they return to the very people who are to blame.

While the public may think of abusers as out of control, unpredictable, and erratic, the opposite is often true. Mixing psychological, emotional, and physical abuse with times of perceived love, happiness, and acceptance is a calculated way for an abuser to gain control and mastery over the victim.

Any enforcer capable of this abuse is ruthless, callous, and inhumane, and such was the nature of Hutu Power, an ideology that sought preservation of power and control among Hutu elites and subjugation of the Tutsis. This ideology had a dual objective: to convince the Hutu masses that they were justified, even duty-bound, to discriminate against all Tutsis, and to convince Tutsis that they were deserving of that discrimination.

Like a spousal abuse perpetrator, they succeeded on both fronts.

POST-REVOLUTION RWANDA

As the birth of an already tired nation rolled into the sixties, it saw guerrilla invasions from neighbouring countries. Tutsis who had been exiled after the revolution attempted to reclaim their country, and the Hutu administration responded brutally towards its Tutsi citizens. In 1963 alone, more than 13,000 people, mostly Tutsis, were killed.

Western nations began to call for more democracy. Gregoire Kayibanda, Rwanda's first elected president, promised to redeem the nation through economic strength and aggressive foreign policy, deliberately ignoring the increasing violence against Tutsis by his own administration. He established a quota system in secondary and university classes, giving Tutsis fewer than 10 percent of the seats. That system also stretched into the civil sphere as Rwanda's top jobs went to Hutus. For all of his efforts, Kayibanda's days as head of state were numbered. He was defeated in a coup by his army chief of staff.

The overthrow of President Kayibanda in 1973 by Juvénal Habyarimana caused cautious optimism. He promised to abolish the quota system in an attempt to stabilize the country and give it a better standing on the world stage. Although opposed by many in the Hutu government, Habyarimana successfully abolished the discriminatory law. However, pressure in his own administration and false cries of Tutsi overrepresentation in education and jobs continued to rise, so he caved, and policies highly favouring Hutus returned.

HATE SPEECH

In 1990 the Kinyarwanda-French magazine *Kangura* was established in Kigali by a Hutu Power extremist named Hassan Ngeze. *Kangura,* which means "wake others up," had a mandate to promote ethnic violence against the Tutsi people and openly called for their extermination. The magazine became a tireless recruiter to the Hutu Power ideology and played a major role in stoking generational hate against the Tutsis by pushing an alternate reality where the Tutsis were the oppressors in the land and had to be vanquished.

In their alternate reality, the Tutsis owned everything, controlled everything, and, like the proverbial wizard behind the curtain, pulled the levers of power against the Hutus to subjugate them as they had in colonial days. The Hutus believed that the social revolution of the early sixties had not succeeded as well as they had hoped. The magazine claimed that the Tutsis had quickly regrouped and through cunning and co-operation managed to occupy the ruling positions of politician, teacher, businessman, and clergy. Soon they would have enough strength to mount a counter-revolution and enslave Hutus once again. The magazine even championed the colonial-era rhetoric that the Belgians had brought to Rwanda, citing nose length and skin colour as proof that the Tutsis had Caucasian ancestry and were therefore the superior race.

As preposterous and outrageous as the propaganda was, it had worked in 1959, 1962, and 1972. Anti-Tutsi propaganda had succeeded in setting parts of the country aflame, ending in the massacre of hundreds of Tutsis. The propagandist magazine and its editors understood that if they could dehumanize the Tutsi people—convince people that they were a nuisance, mere cockroaches that had to be exterminated—they could appeal to the uneducated youth, a segment of the population that needed vision and work.

Also legitimizing *Kangura's* fake news was that the Rwandan Patriotic Front (RPF), the exiled refugees of the revolution who had grown in strength and now commanded a solid military force, kept attacking from Uganda in the north. As retaliation, the Rwandan military punished Tutsis inside their border, killing their own people. *Kangura* sought to blur the lines between the RPF and the civilian Tutsis living in Rwanda.

To its readers, both were one and the same, and both needed to be dealt with.

Kangura did this during a time of poverty when education, healthcare, and employment were difficult to obtain. It convinced the public that Tutsis had succeeded in staging their silent coup and were behind the decline of the nation. So *Kangura*, after setting the bleakest of scenes, had a solution: Hutus had to unite and overturn the current order. The role of *Kangura* and other propaganda media outlets that would later follow was clear: to prepare the way for the coming onslaught.

The constant psychological agenda that was uninterrupted by an opposing voice framed the mindset of many Tutsis and kept them paralyzed. When the RPF would stage an attack and the Tutsis in Kigali were punished for it, they would turn and blame the RPF, which was attempting to liberate them, instead of the government that was suppressing them, just as an abuse victim will turn on herself, blaming herself for what the perpetrator is doing. Such was the success of this psychological warfare that the Rwandan army even staged a fake attack on Kigali, then arrested and killed many Tutsis, saying that the RPF had reached the capital city. Many Tutsis living in Rwanda accepted whatever came to them as just life as a Tutsi in Rwanda and resigned themselves to the fact that this was perhaps the way it would always be. Our maid even tried to convince Charity to pretend she was Hutu to shield her from potential danger. The government, aided by the hate media machine in Rwanda, was succeeding in the psychological warfare. Armed warfare would soon follow.

In December 1990, *Kangura* published the infamous Hutu Ten Commandments, which became the rallying cry for Hutu Power extremism. The Hutu Ten Commandments stated,

1. Every Hutu must know that the Tutsi woman, wherever she may be, is working for the Tutsi ethnic cause. In consequence, any Hutu is a traitor who
    — acquires a Tutsi wife
    — acquires a Tutsi concubine
    — acquires a Tutsi secretary or protégée.
2. Every Hutu must know that our Hutu daughters are more worthy and more conscientious as women, as wives and as mothers. Aren't they lovely, excellent secretaries, and more honest!
3. Hutu women, be vigilant and make sure that your husbands, brothers and sons see reason.
4. All Hutus must know that all Tutsis are dishonest in business. Their only goal is ethnic superiority. We have learned this by experience from experience. In consequence, any Hutu is a traitor who
    — forms a business alliance with a Tutsi
    — invests his own funds or public funds in a Tutsi enterprise
    — borrows money from or loans money to a Tusti
    — grants favours to Tutsis (import licences, bank loans, land for construction, public markets...)
5. Strategic positions such as politics, administration, economics, the military and security must be restricted to the Hutu.
6. A Hutu majority must prevail throughout the educational system (pupils, scholars, teachers).
7. The Rwandan army must be exclusively Hutu. The war of October 1990 has taught us that. No soldier may marry a Tutsi woman.

8. Hutu must stop taking pity on the Tutsi.
9. Hutu wherever they be must stand united, in solidarity, and concerned with the fate of their Hutu brothers. Hutu within and without Rwanda must constantly search for friends and allies to the Hutu cause, beginning with their Bantu brothers.

    Hutu must constantly counter Tutsi propaganda.

    Hutu must stand firm and vigilant against their common enemy: the Tutsi.
10. The social revolution of 1959, the Referendum of 1961 and the Hutu Ideology must be taught to Hutu of every age. Every Hutu must spread the word wherever he goes. Any Hutu who persecutes his brother Hutu for spreading and teaching this ideology is a traitor.

In 1993, another stronghold for Hutu Power was established when Radio Television Libre Mille Collines (RTLM) was created, and although it only broadcasted for thirteen months, it had devastating consequences. Funded by the Habyarimana administration, it preached messages of hate and discrimination against Tutsis, moderate Hutus, and even Belgians. When some people, including the Belgian ambassador, sought Western help to shut down the broadcasts, it was dismissed as a joke. David Rawson, US ambassador in 1993, said the messages were open to interpretation and that the US believed in free speech.

A Harvard study showed that 9.9 percent of genocidal participation was because of the radio station, and 51,000 deaths are attributed to it as hosts and broadcasters alerted the Hutu extremists of the location of Tutsi people. The battle cry of every Hutu extremist blared loud and clear from RTLM on April 6, 1994, the day of the genocide. It was coded but the meaning could not be mistaken: "cut down the tall trees."

Chapter 6
LIGHT IN THE DARKNESS

DARLING

EUROPE WAS AN ADVENTURE. THACIENNE WAS ENROLLED IN A BIBLE school while Alphonse completed his practicum at a local charismatic Baptist church. After they were wed, their focus turned to how they wanted to begin their life together in ministry. Alphonse began to work his sources in Africa for ministries opportunities. The conflict that had driven him out of Rwanda made him resist a return to his native land. A promising position in Burundi fell through, then one in Madagascar. Rwanda suddenly became the only viable option. The young Karuhijes set aside three days to pray to make certain what they were receiving in their hearts, and the answer was clear: Rwanda.

They landed in Kigali, their life's trajectory now set. Alphonse and Thacienne were different from the teenagers they had been when tribalism forced them to flee. There was no animosity, and they were not jaded, but they had returned with a sense of purpose: Rwanda would be the operating base where God would use them to shake the forces of darkness. Tutsi notwithstanding, God had prepared them for such a time as they were in to make a mark that could not be erased.

With no large platform and limited resources, Alphonse, who was fluent in both Kinyarwanda and English, managed to secure a job translating classic Christian literature and hymnal books from English to Kinyarwanda. They settled down in a poor area of Kigali, and soon Patrick was born to them. Two years later, Charity came into the world. Yet even with the rapid growth of the Karuhije family, all that was in Alphonse's heart was to bring knowledge of Jesus to a country whose racial tension was boiling over. He quickly recognized that if he was going to be able to truly impact Rwanda, it had to begin in his own community, where many people were open to the gospel. Knowing no other way to engage his neighbours, Alphonse began a Bible study group in his home, and what began with a modest number of locals meeting for prayer and Bible study burst into a mini revival that shook the little neighbourhood as more and more people were continually added.

But it was not their passion for the gospel that first drew the attention of their neighbours. It was their genuine love for each other. Their modest home was void of the luxury of a modern stove, and Alphonse would help Thacienne draw water from the local well and bring it in their backyard, where they would cook their meals over an open fire. Their open-air kitchen allowed ample exposure to their perplexed neighbours, who could not fathom why the man was taking part in the duties that clearly belonged to the woman!

As they worked and laughed together, often singing, Alphonse frequently looked at Thacienne and call her his darling.

"My darling Thacienne," he would say in his unique baritone voice, which I still hear to this day. The curious neighbours, continuing to observe this strange European couple who just happened to have black skin, were unfamiliar with the word "darling" and decided it had to be one of Thacienne's name. But when they heard Thacienne using it for Alphonse, it became less likely! In wonderment of how fond Alphonse was of his wife, a woman asked Thacienne one day, "What do you do for your man that makes him treat you so well?" That light caused people to be curious about Alphonse and Thacienne, and that curiosity turned into attraction as many began to fill their Bible study.

When they eventually purchased a larger home in that same community, tens of people turned to hundreds of people, and the sounds of prayer and worship spilled into the streets. Even people walking past the home found themselves drawn inside and participating in the services. Farmers, peasants, beggars, and prostitutes continued to come until even local businessmen and politicians began to attend. At first it was fascination—what was this man teaching that was drawing such crowds into his home? But it was not long before they too were raising their hands and asking for prayer. The numbers increased to where Alphonse had to tear down walls to accommodate the people.

It was not that Alphonse had a special ability to attract crowds; people came to hear him and take part in the community of believers because of the uncompromised Word of God that was being shared. It was not tainted with religiosity and politics like many churches at that time were. The message was without prejudice and partiality, relevant both to the Tutsi and the Hutu.

Jesus in the same way attracted people by the thousands! At many points in His ministry, there was no room to stand or to get through to just catch a glimpse of Him. Israel bubbled with the news of this man who taught with such authority. This message of the hope and grace found in His kingdom was distant from the oppression of the Roman government in power and foreign to the religious authority of the Sanhedrin. Jesus taught it with such conviction, causing men and women to be persuaded that perhaps they could take part in it. And as they did, the blind received sight, the dead were raised, the lame walked, and the poor had the hope of this kingdom proclaimed to them.

In much the same way, in Alphonse and Thacienne's thriving ministry many wanted to know what God's Word said regarding many issues in their lives. They were tired of the divisive message that permeated everyday Rwanda. It was not just apologists of the Habyarimana regime who preached Hutu Power in all its shapes and forms. Pastors and clergymen became some of the biggest supporters of the ideology, exchanging the impartial purity of the gospel for extreme philosophies of men. What the soul of man truly hungers for was not being found in many churches, but it was being found in the home of a young Tutsi couple. Miracles took place, people were baptized in the Holy Spirit, salvation abounded, and for four years the kingdom of heaven flickered like light in the darkness in that little neighbourhood in Kigali.

In 1983, Alphonse and Thacienne returned to England for Alphonse to complete his seminary training in Trinity Theological College in Bristol. The Karuhijes then moved to Paris. In 1987 they returned to Rwanda, where Alphonse oversaw various projects, helping ministries build schools, church buildings, offices, and other projects. The family had grown from four to six after I was born in England and Benjamin was born in France.

ROYAL REFUGEES

Many years ago I watched a film titled *Life Is Beautiful*. The Italian director, Roberto Benigni, also starred in it. The heart-wrenching movie went on to win several awards, including three Academy Awards, for its emotional portrayal of a Jewish family living in Italy during World War II. In this moving story that begins in 1939, a Jewish man named Guido Orifice arrives in what was then the kingdom of Italy and with his charm and humour wins the affections of a local woman named Dora, who was engaged to a wealthy but arrogant man. Guido and Dora are instead married. Together they run a bookstore, and later they have a son named Giosue. All seems just right, but their perfect life is interrupted by the outbreak of World War II. Guido and Giosue are arrested on Giosue's birthday and are sent to a concentration camp. Dora volunteers to go with them to be close to her husband and son, but when they arrive men and women are separated. In the camp, Guido shields his son from the horror of their situation by creating a game. He explains to his son that whoever gets to one thousand points by performing various tasks around the camp will win a tank. With people dying all around them from bullets and gas chambers, Guido is able to preserve his son's spirit and innocence by maintaining the ruse, remaining in character until the very end when Allied soldiers arrive to liberate the camp at the end of the war. In the touching last scene, Guido places his son in a box, assuring him that remaining in the box until everyone is gone is the final challenge, and runs off to find his wife. Guido is caught by a German guard, who decides to execute him, and as he is being marched past the box that Giosue is hiding in, Guido, still in character, winks at his son. Giosue winks back, unaware that his father is being led to his death. The next morning, Giosue emerges from his hiding place just as a US Army unit led by a tank is passing by. The camp is liberated and the prisoners set free, and Giosue is reunited with his mother, Dora. When Giosue is older, he realizes the astonishing sacrifices his father had made in protecting him from the horrors of the Holocaust.

Such was my life growing up in the ticking time bomb that Rwanda had become. While many parents taught their children to either hate the Tutsi and love the Hutu or pity the Tutsi and honour the Hutu, we were taught to love people the way Jesus did, and loving our enemies became what our family was known for.

A large family was frequently in want, with not enough food for all the children. My dad routinely visited them to see how they were doing and took rice and whatever was needed to them. One day, the father in the family was overheard ridiculing and insulting my father. "That Alphonse," he said, "someone should take him out!" He was Hutu. It was brought to the attention of my father, who had a very unusual reaction. Upon hearing the news, he bellowed out his signature laughter and exclaimed, "If he kills me, who is going to feed him rice?" Dad went on bringing them food and taking care of them, and the matter was settled.

On other occasions, he would willingly pay for the education of children whose parents hated us. He practised the golden rule, doing good to others as we would have them do unto us, to the very people who wanted us destroyed as Tutsi cockroaches.

While the "Tutsi vs Hutu" narrative continued to permeate Rwandan culture through politics, education, business, and religious life, this was the culture I grew up in. Sure, our lives were continually in danger, assassination attempts on my parents were made, many times we would not go to school without a security escort, and every available voice roared with propaganda, but, like Giosue, I was blissfully unaware of the breaking down of the world around me. I was never taught to see Tutsi or Hutu. Instead, I was taught to frame my reality and my mindset with the teaching of the Bible. Being older, I now understand that the continued favour and success my parents enjoyed in the midst of a divided country were based on what they knew about God— that He shows no partiality, while the world around them did. I still remember the worn-out well-used Bible they kept. Of the many verses they held dear, Psalm 91 was dearest to my mother, as it was the chapter that assured her we would be kept safe from the genocide that was coming. "*A thousand may fall at your side,*" the seventh verse says, "*ten thousand at your right hand, but it will not come near you. You will only look with your eyes and see the recompense of the wicked.*"

While it was extremely difficult for a Tutsi to rise in the high ranks of ministry influence, my father grew in favour with the right people and continually saw promotion, even being elected bishop. He was able to accumulate wealth for his family through enterprise and to break barriers as a Tutsi in a Hutu-dominated world. He produced enough income to hire maids and live-in nannies as he and my mom constantly travelled. We frequently dined and played in the best hotels in Rwanda, and we even attended private schools, with my older brother Patrick being sent to boarding school in Belgium. As we continued to prosper as a family, envy and jealousy were stoked in our enemies, and harassment came hard and fast. Yet we pressed on, refusing to succumb to the distorted image that others had of Tutsis. Throughout the intimidation and threats levelled at my parents, they refused to hate their oppressors, but they equally refused to let us children believe that we were victims of racism. We belonged to God and were made in His image, and God did not have victims; He only had children.

As Giosue looked upon a Nazi concentration camp and saw a game, I looked upon the ticking time bomb that was Rwanda and saw my home. Nazis and Jews in Giosue's eyes were characters playing roles, and Hutus and Tutsis were people who lived in my home. Tutsis were not cockroaches but people who deserved God's love, just as Hutus were not enemies but people whom God loved. As for me, I was a child of God, and though I do not remember my parents calling me it, I was royalty. Years later, one of my younger brothers, Ben, talked to our mom about how she had raised us to think that we were royalty and never less than anyone else. Even when we lost everything and sought asylum as refugees in Kenya and later immigrated to Canada with hardly anything to our name, we had an unshakable confidence in God's ability to rescue us and get us through the overwhelming circumstances. Despite everything that we would eventually go through, there remained, buried in our subconscious, the overcoming mentality placed there by our parents that we were never less than anyone else. Our mother looked at Ben and said, "That is what I have always wanted." That mindset is what kept us hopeful despite the overwhelming odds stacked up against our survival in what was coming.

One would think that a war refugee from a Third World nation after arriving at the opulence of the Western world would suddenly forget the sting of the situation they are leaving behind and have their countenance changed and heart renewed to forge ahead in optimism, but many times the opposite is true. Often there is a struggle to be accepted by the residents of the new world, and prejudice and stereotypes are flung on you that can be daunting to overcome. Confidence is hard to achieve as everything you once knew is no longer relevant. That was not the case for us. We adjusted quickly and fluidly, unhampered by thoughts of insecurity or inferiority. God still did not show partiality for one people over the other, whether they were Hutu or Tutsi or African or Western. We were refugees, yes, but we were also taught that we were children of God and therefore royalty. We were royal refugees.

Chapter 7
THE GREAT ESCAPE

WHEN MOM AND DAD RETURNED TO RWANDA IN 1989, THEY WENT BACK to a very different place than they had left six years earlier. Like the calm duck that seems to float effortlessly across the pond, Rwanda looked relatively calm, but underneath, the stage for the historic tragedy was being set. The collapse of coffee trade, which was one of Rwanda's greatest exports, caused a major hit to the economy, adding fuel to what was already a tense time. But worse yet, rumours abounded of the Rwandan army training a brutal militia known as Interahamwe. In the early 90s, the civil unrest of the nation caught momentum, and the old winds of destruction began to blow.

UP AND DOWN

With the RPF's attacks on the Rwandan army continuing, the government took advantage of the situation, purchased a large supply of machetes, and supplied the Rwandan public with them. The justification for the mass distribution of arms was convenient: should they fail to have enough military troops to protect the citizenry from the mounting threat of the RPF, the machetes could be used by the civilians in self-defence.

One of the most vivid memories I have of growing up is standing outside our side door that led to the backyard, watching the butchering of a chicken from beginning to end. Pekosi, one of our servants, would take the chicken by the legs and stretch its body over a piece of wood. Down would come the machete, severing the head from the body. Then the autonomic nervous system of the chicken would take over, adrenaline would rush into it, and for a few minutes the poor chicken ran headless around our backyard. One stroke from the machete is all it took.

That was easy compared to butchering cattle. After the animal was killed came the hard part—cutting and preparing the meat. The butcher with all his strength made several blows to the heavy piece of meat and needed rest before proceeding. Up and down the machete went—the skilled butcher had the monotonous action down to a routine, a slow winding of the arm upwards and a swift stroke downward as the flesh continued to give way. It was work, a term that the Interahamwe particularly relished. *Intera* comes from the Rwandese word for "work" and *hamwe* for "together": *interahamwe*. What the butcher did to the cow, so the Hutus would do the Tutsis, "work" being the industry of genocide. From the early 50s, when state-sponsored killing of Tutsis by Hutus began, the massacres were referred to as work—simply clearing the bush.

The machete was the most widely used weapon in the genocide, and perhaps the most intimate (except rape) for the proximity to the victim it took to kill. As with the butcher with the cattle—the slow winding of the arm upwards and a swift stroke down—several blows would have to be landed on the victim. Attackers would take shifts, unable to endure the repetitive task of "up and down" for very long.

THE WALKING DEAD

The Interahamwe boasted of being able to kill a thousand Tutsis in only twenty minutes. Trucks carrying the rowdy group could be seen around Rwanda even before the genocide, but they did not yet kill in the open. Drunk from alcohol and RTLM propaganda that blared from the portable radios they carried, they harassed Tutsi women in marketplaces and intimidated their husbands on the streets. They looked leaderless, wore no uniforms, and carried no ranks. A foreigner to Rwanda might look upon them and see only a disorderly and raucous bunch, disturbing the peace and nothing more. But that's only what they did in public.

At almost forty different sites outside the Rwandan capital, the paramilitary group was perfecting the craft of mass slaughter. They trained with the Rwandan army, learning how to kill with cruelty and no remorse, the machete being their weapon of choice. The disciplines of unity and cohesiveness dominated their training, and they were fuelled by unbridled hate for the Tutsi, whom they regarded as animals—subhuman. To these purveyors of the Hutu Power ideology, Tutsis were cockroaches, and their task, their duty, was to exterminate them. They were trained to believe in a fundamental right to torture and kill any Tutsi they encountered, going beyond murder to barbarianism. They would later be called *abantu bapfuye bahagaze*, translated as "men who are dead yet stand"; they were the walking dead.

What seemed like a mob of drunk soccer fanatics was a group of men who were inwardly calculating, waiting for the signal that would unleash organized terrorism with precision and focus. They trained to work together as one engine of genocide, a perfect killing machine.

Meanwhile an opposing force had amassed in Uganda, the Rwandan Patriotic Force, made up of Rwandan refugees who had fled during the Rwandan Revolution of 1959. Since that time, they had not been recognized as true Rwandan citizens and had been forcibly denied entry by both the Kayibanda and Habyarimana regimes. But the discrimination they experienced was the very thing that bonded them, and they were driven by a common goal, a recognition of citizenship and an end to identification cards and ethnic prejudice.

They were 5,000 men strong when they attacked Rwanda from the north through Uganda in October 1990. Buoyed by the element of surprise, they advanced sixty kilometres deep to the town of Gabiro, but they were eventually driven back when Zaire and France intervened to assist the Rwandan armed forces. Struck down but not entirely destroyed, the RPF regrouped and mounted an aggressive recruiting campaign. By early 1994, they had gone from a regiment of 5,000 men to a corps of 25,000 soldiers.

GLIMPSES OF HEAVEN

As things in Rwanda intensified and the genocide advanced with each passing day, I personally began to witness that same divine protection that had been with my mom and dad when they escaped Rwanda in their youth, almost as a foreshadow of what would soon be coming.

It was 1990 and I was six years old when we were told that the RPF had reached Kigali. But it was all a ruse. The increasingly desperate Habyarimana regime was slowly losing credibility with foreign nations as a democratic state, and the outcry increased for them to reach a peace agreement with the RPF. To gain back some control of the narrative, they staged a fake war in the nation's capital, complete with explosions and gunfire, all in an effort to persuade the country's citizens, as well as the world, that the RPF was dangerous and now formidable enough to achieve its aim of recapturing Rwanda and taking it back to the colonial-era days of Hutu subjugation. Habyarimana then used the supposed attack as a pretext to arrest thousands of prominent Tutsis, already on a list, accusing them of colluding with the terrorist state of the RPF. Among the many Tutsis the military came for was my dad.

That night, I was woken by a loud sound that sent fear like a shockwave through my body. Even living in Rwanda, I had not grown accustomed to gunfire, especially in the suburbs of Kigali where we lived. But the sound was unmistakable. Not only was someone shooting at us; we were also surrounded.

My hands groped in the dark, looking for anything to shield myself as my head swam. Then someone pounced on me, picked me up, and ran with me, whispering for me to remain silent. It was my dad. Flanked by the rest of the family we quietly slipped out the back door and raced to our neighbours' house. We stayed with them for a few days as things in Kigali quieted down. An attempt had been made, but we had slipped away from it unscathed and undetected, a highly improbable outcome. It was reported that during those two days 10,000 Tutsis and Hutu moderates were arrested and 348 killed. We were not among them.

In those days, it was not shocking for Tutsis to disappear. I remember leaving the house on a morning when I didn't have school to play with some neighbourhood friends. We spotted an old abandoned Volkswagen Beetle about fifty feet from my house. I remembered that I had heard some gunshots during the night. My friends and I approached it and noticed that the glass had been pierced by a sharp object. Peering in, we saw that the inside of the car was splattered with blood, but there was no body. I remember just staring at the red spray over the upholstery but not fearing it, almost as if it was no big deal. I realize today how traumatic that would be for a child, yet I was unmoved, as if it were a regular occurrence and no cause for alarm. My parents had come home one day with their car punctured by bullet holes. This was life for a Tutsi. We had lived under the threats to life for so long that death was not odd; rather it was normal, almost accepted.

But although there was regular discrimination and random killing of Tutsis, there was something else, something more sinister and deliberate, that pervaded the air around Rwanda. Like the calm within the eye of the storm, there was an anticipation, an unease about something. It seemed like things were finally coming to a head. Another assassination attempt was made on my family.

Dad had been elected as the bishop of Kibungo Diocese in Ngoma district in the Eastern Province of Rwanda. There was an uproar among Hutu religious leaders about a Tutsi man holding such a prominent religious position, especially after defeating a Hutu candidate in the election process. Nonetheless, we made plans to leave Kigali for our new home in Kibungo, where Dad would be serving, wisely sending an aide ahead. The news we received before moving showed how deep the prejudicial hate had seeped into the church.

An elaborate plot had been devised for the assassination of our entire family. It was so meticulously planned that we would not have seen the light of day had we come close to anywhere in the Eastern Province. Dad stepped down from his new position and a Hutu man was given the post, but the message was clear: not even in the church were Tutsis safe.

WORLDS APART

My mom became troubled and quickly arrived at the conclusion that we would not be safe if we stayed in Kigali. It recalled the same thoughts and feelings her father, Anastase, had before making the decision to flee Rwanda decades earlier. The gentle and meek Thacienne became a bulldog, and clinging to her Bible she aggressively petitioned heaven for safety for her family. I have a vivid memory of being woken in the middle of the night by Mom's uncharacteristically loud, aggressive praying. Out of Psalm 91:7, she prayed, "A thousand may fall at your side, ten thousand at your right hand, but it will not come near you."

But for all that had happened, Dad was worlds apart from Mom and her continual insistence to leave. Not only did he not want to leave his congregation in dire times; he also held hope that the peace negotiations President Habyarimana was holding with the RPF under UN supervision would lead to relative peace. The UN had dispatched the United Nations Assistance Mission for Rwanda (UNAMIR), which would see 2,500 troops in Rwanda oversee the signing and keeping of the Arusha Accords, an agreement to end the ongoing civil war between the Rwandan government and the RPF. Surely nothing would happen in the presence of the UN peacekeeping corps, and certainly not with the international attention the UN was bringing to the situation! Dad agreed to leave only if he sensed God telling him that he had to, so Mom prayed that God would intervene and allow him to be privy to the persistence she felt in her heart that they must leave, and leave now.

One day, Dad met a member of the RPF who confirmed that indeed something big was about to happen and it would be wise for him to leave quickly. This report, coupled with Mom's plea, convinced Dad. Tanzania was the most logical place to go, as it was close by and Thacienne's family lived there, but it would mean that they would be driving through Ngoma district and perhaps through Kibungo, the place where months earlier a trap had been set for our assassination.

UNDER HIS SHADOW

On Tuesday, March 29, 1994, Mom woke me up at 3 o'clock in the morning. This was it—our escape under cover of darkness, a surreal repeat of her escape into Burundi as a child. We left the caretaking of our home to our two housekeepers, assuring them, as we had told everyone else, that we were only visiting family in Tanzania over Easter. People knew Thacienne had family there, and there was nothing suspicious about our trip, but we still held to the cover of darkness, especially as we would be passing through Kibungo, forty-five miles from Kigali. If we were to be noticed anywhere in the country, that would be the place.

As we approached Kibungo, prayer arose from the driver and front-seat passengers. Some of the Interahamwe militia had been planted in this region, and more than a few knew who Alphonse Karuhije was. They were recording names and vehicles, personal or business, and taking photos. But as we drove through, we saw a ghost town. There was no one in sight, no sentries posted, no farmers rising early for chores—nothing. In the car, prayer turned to praise. Heaven was at it again, and our confidence in God buoyed us as we approached the border between Rwanda and Tanzania.

As we approached the gate, a large barrel-chested military officer with an AK-47 slung from his right shoulder waved our vehicle forward. Prayers from the driver and front-seat passengers began again, but quieter this time, as our 1993 Peugeot Turbo sedan crept ahead. Peering through the windshield as he approached, the officer instantly recognized Tutsis and barked for our identification cards. As Dad found the documents, Mom's mind raced with any reason she could give as to why a Tutsi family of seven, crammed in a five-passenger vehicle, would be leaving the country in the early hours of the morning.

He didn't ask. He stared at our ID cards as if trying to make sense of something, peered at us with another peculiar look on his face, then looked again at the ID cards. Then, with a gruff nod to the gatekeeper, he handed back our ID cards and waved us through.

A SAD PARTING

After narrowly escaping from Rwanda, what greeted us on the other side of the border was the rough and raw terrain of west Tanzania. Our hardy Peugeot soldiered through pothole, ditch, and rut to get us through. With the region's reputation of having wildcats hiding in the tall grass, breakdowns were not an option.

We reached the rural town of Bukoba and stayed there a few days. Yet in the back of Dad's mind, return was inevitable.

Mom reminded him of the treason of the church community and its continual attempts on our lives, but Dad remained firm on his decision to not abandon his church members and their families, once again claiming that if God confirmed that he was indeed in danger, he would not return. Mom, on the other hand, maintained that God in fact had spoken through the various close calls and multiple near brushes with death. Dad countered that there had been no indication of an extreme spike in violence in Rwanda, the Arusha Accords were still in effect with international eyes watching, both political sides continued to co-operate to reach a resolution, and as Easter approached, what would it say of a dean and pastor to be MIA?

As Mom helplessly stared at the man she had fallen in love with many years before, she recognized the same fearlessness he had expressed when he asked her to be his, knowing full well that she was betrothed to another. He had won her over then, and he would win now. My dad was returning into the belly of the beast, and despite her best efforts she would not be able to stop him. But what gripped her the most was the unshakable feeling that she would never see him again.

She wouldn't. On April 6, 1994, at around 8:20 p.m. (UTC), the airplane carrying Rwanda's president, Juvénal Habyarimana, and Burundi's president, Cyprien Ntaryamira, approached Kigali International Airport. The Dassault Falcon 50 circled once around the airport before coming in for its final approach. It was a clear night. A surface-to-air missile hit one of the wings, and a second one hit the tail, sending the presidential jet spiralling in the sky before crashing in the garden of the presidential palace, killing everyone on board.

Chapter 8
THE WALKING DEAD

HEAVEN'S AGENT

WHEN THE PRESIDENTIAL PLANE WAS SHOT DOWN ON THAT APRIL evening, Thacienne understood that Hutu extremists all over Rwanda had been waiting for that proverbial straw that would break the camel's back. This was it. It reeked of much more than a coincidence; it seemed more an opportunity. The propaganda tools Radio Television Libre des Mille Collines and Radio Rwanda roared to life with calls to exterminate the Tutsis in the "final war." The call to arms for the Interahamwe and Hutu extremists was a simple coded message, "Cut down the tall trees." This phrase was carried on by major media outlets immediately following the crash.

The culprit behind the missile attack would never be caught. The guilty party, whether Hutu or Tutsi, would never be definitively determined. Most blamed Hutu extremists as the architect of the attack, a forced domino effect that would finally bring about what they had desired the most. Some blame the RPF and its then leader Paul Kagame. A noted BBC correspondent who was in Rwanda during the genocide commented how the source of the assassination could turn out to be one of the greatest mysteries of the 20th centuries. Whoever the masterminds were, their actions became the catalyst that would change Rwanda and its people forever.

By this time Alphonse had returned to Rwanda, and we were lodging in an inn, waiting for him to return. Thacienne didn't know what to think or what to do, being miles away in Tanzania, anxiously anticipating the return of her husband. She could sense the collective gasp of a nation and a people about to go through their apocalypse, but her thoughts remained centred on one person. She would have given anything to be with him and protect him from what was about to take place. Alphonse was not just another man; he had become a successful, prosperous Tutsi who was now well-known, and this made him even more of a target. He would be hunted down. There would no longer be a safe place for him to hide. The very people he would typically go to for sanctuary would be the ones who would now plot against him. Thacienne knew all this, and she wept for him. Thoughts snowballed into fears as questions she had no answer for descended on her like the heavy African rain. What would become of her and her children? Would they remain in this inn until he came back? What if he could not return? Did they have enough money to survive?

When the great Hebrew prophet Elijah was in danger of starvation because of the drought in the land, God said to him, "Arise, go to Zarephath, which belongs to Sidon, and dwell there. Behold, I have commanded a widow there to feed you" (1 Kings

17:9). God is known in the Scriptures and throughout history as Jehovah Jireh, the God who sees ahead and provides. Elijah's widow was able to take care of him, and in turn she was blessed. Our "widow" was a man named Eugene, a Roman Catholic minister who lived in a beautiful residence close to where we waited in Ganta. Before leaving for Rwanda, Alphonse had been introduced to him once. Alphonse had made Eugene promise him that he would take care of his family were he not to return. When the winds of the genocide blew the hardest, we were safe in Eugene's residence, unaware of and unscathed by the horrors that were transpiring across the border. For eight months he fed us, clothed us, and took care of us, yet for all the gratitude that we showered on him for his abundant generosity, our gratitude was first directed to heaven. We were not forgotten.

THE FIRST MASSACRE

Gikondo had a strong Hutu extremist influence and naturally became the site of the first mass killing, triggering a wave of violence that enveloped the nation. On April 9, three days after the death of President Habyarimana, the killing had already begun, but not in the way it was about take place in the Pallotine Missionary Catholic compound, which included a church ran by Polish priests. What was about to happen would set a standard for a quicker path to exterminating the inyenzi—a more efficient genocide.

Tutsis fearing for their lives naturally fled for sanctuary at the Catholic church, and the clergy did their best to accommodate and protect the people. Roadblocks had already been set up to catch fleeing Tutsis, including one near the church, but as many Tutsis arrived, the Interahamwe occupying the roadblocks simply let them pass and walk into the compound. Why waste their energy on creating unnecessary havoc when all the Tutsis would soon be in one place?

More than 100 Tutsis filled the church and compound, and presidential guard soldiers were first to arrive. They checked all identity cards, urged all Hutus to leave, and forced Tutsis to stay in the church. When the priests protested that they were all church members, they were told that they were guilty of harbouring inyenzi. The soldiers decided to not waste their bullets. "The Interahamwe will soon be coming."

Shortly after, they came. Even before they reached the church, you could hear them as they marched into the compound, one hundred strong, chanting their war songs, intoxicated and inebriated, ready for work. The killing did not stop for two straight hours. Sparing no bullet, they hacked, clubbed, and mutilated Tutsis with perversity and swiftness, taking special care to leave none alive. They returned a few days later to look for survivors, and finding injured victims that had taken refuge in another building, they doused the building in gas and lit it on fire. The screams died quickly. The smoke saw to that. The victims' identity cards were taken and burned so none could be identified.

Over a thousand Tutsis took refuge in a church in Musha, a village in Rwanda. It is said that the "work" there took 12 hours, from 8 a.m. to 8 p.m., and finally ended when the church was lit on fire with the survivors inside. When the Interahamwe arrived at any place where there were large numbers of Tutsis, they killed to the extent their strength would allow, slit the Achilles heels of whoever was still alive to prevent escape, then rested for a few hours. When they awoke, they finished the "work."

In Rubavu district in the Western Province of Rwanda, Hutu extremists arrived as false friends. They encouraged Tutsis living there to follow them to where they would be safe and protected. Two years before, the government had ordered the prisoners of Gisenyi Prison to dig a large hole. They could not have known that two years later it would be used as a mass grave for the living. The Tutsis who answered the call to go to safety were buried alive in that hole. Hands flailing, they wept, and their voices were eventually drowned beneath the sand that covered them.

Yet this was just the beginning. With brutality and swiftness, the Interahamwe swept through the country with coordinated precision and cruelty, going through checklists of the names of almost every Tutsi who lived in the rural areas. If the list was incorrect, they relied on local Hutu allies for information. The slave master of tribalism drove them to not only murder but mutilate, torture, and rape their victims.

CHILDREN OF BAD MEMORIES

They were called "Enfants Mauvaise Souvenir," Children of Bad Memory, and they numbered in the thousands. These were children conceived by rape.

If years of Hutu Power propaganda was the seed, the genocide was the harvest, and the fruits it bore were multi-faceted but had one end goal: the complete annihilation of the Tutsis. The Hutus employed various weapons like rifles and machetes, but perhaps the most devastating was the weapon of rape.

Hundreds of thousands of Tutsi women were subjected to unspeakable sexual violence at the hands of the Interahamwe, the Rwandan armed forces, and even other civilians. Research after the genocide revealed that nearly all women over twelve years of age were raped individually or gang-raped, and many were taken as sex slaves. The bodies of children as young as six or seven years old were discovered, swollen and split. They had been gang-raped and killed. UN Special Rapporteur Rene Degni-Segui would later say, "Rape was the rule, and its absence the exception."

Hutu extremists continued to encourage what would later be termed "genocidal rape"—mass rape used as an act of genocide—used first in the Yugoslav Wars and the Rwanda genocide. It was a coordinated and deliberate strategy against the Tutsi, a pure weapon. The extremists understood that while weapons destroy the body, rape destroys the soul of not only the victim but the community and the people as a whole. The ploy was to continually dehumanize the Tutsi people so that they would see themselves the way Hutu extremists saw them, as inyenzis...cockroaches.

So the depravity worsened as the militia, in particular, went to extreme lengths to degrade Tutsi women. Rape became part of a pattern to destroy the soul and spirit of their victims. After looting and ransacking the homes of Tutsi families, the Interahamwe took the women, many grandmothers, mothers, and daughters, and raped them while their families were forced to watch. If they did not release the victimized women, they would kill them, then their families, sometimes reversing the order.

Hundreds of HIV patients were released from the hospital during the conflicts to travel around the country as "rape squads," spreading the awful disease among Tutsi women. Many survivors detailed how after being severely raped multiple times, they were released and told they would die of shame and sadness, if AIDS did not kill them first.

I struggle to write this even now as I picture the women in my life—my wife, my mother, my sister. The words Jesus Christ used to describe Satan ring in my mind: "The thief comes only to steal and kill and destroy" (John 10:10). It was not that God had abandoned Rwanda, as many concluded, but that the leaders of the nation had relinquished their rule and authority to such deep darkness and emptied their souls of light. Cardinal Roger Etchegaray, visiting Rwanda on behalf of the pope, asked if the blood of tribalism ran deeper than the waters of baptism. A Rwandan religious leader answered, "Yes." But for my dad, no amount of terror would cause Him to abandon the One whom he loved, and no terror could convince him that the One who also loved him had abandoned him. Stuck behind enemy lines, his mission was clear: save as many as he could.

THE WALKING DEAD
Still, it was impossible for him not to hear the screams on that horrific first night. More than 8,000 would be killed. As the Western nations evacuated their citizens, the first Rwandans slaughtered were moderate Hutu politicians. They had refused to co-operate with the Hutu Power agenda, and they would pay the price. Lieutenant-General Roméo Dallaire, the UNAMIR leader and a Canadian, called the UN, urging them to intervene in the massacre that was taking place. He is told to stand down and not to get involved in any armed conflict.

Anakleti, the youngest of Thacienne's siblings, and my uncle, was in Rwanda when the genocide began. Thacienne had done all she could to get him to come with us to Tanzania, but his complacency prevented his departure. Anakleti, a well-known man in his village, had a pet dog that he was particularly attached to. It was very rare to find Anakleti in the marketplace, in the fields, or even on the roads without his best friend tagging along beside him.

After hearing of the devastation in Kigali, he took all he could to survive, including his dog, and went into hiding in nearby woods, barricading himself in a man-made pit. When the local Interahamwe rebels came looking him, a neighbour and acquaintance of his told them that if they could find his dog, they would find Anakleti. As they combed through the woods looking for him, Anakleti's faithful friend let out defensive barks, attempting to protect his master, which alerted the militia to where he was hiding. Anakleti was hacked to death alongside his dog.

The brutality of those days was only eclipsed by the shock of having your family and friends give you up for being Tutsi, some for fear of their lives, others out of a perverted sense of patriotism. For many, what stung more than the bloodstained machete cutting through flesh was the cold realization of who was wielding it. As the sun came up during those months, children as young as eight were seen holding a machete in one hand, their other hand clutching their father's hand, as they marched to "work," while others waited expectantly for the latest update on where the inyenzis were hiding from their portable radios tuned in to RTLM.

The radio station that had churned propaganda into an art no longer used covert tactics in expressing their disdain for Tutsis. "Take special care to disembowel pregnant victims," one announcer said. "The graves are not yet full," said another. RTLM continued to give out the precise locations of surviving bands of Tutsis and would give congratulations once the job was finished.

As for Alphonse, the sting was compounded by the fact that it was not just his friends and co-workers who had abandoned him; it was pastors and priests, religious leaders who had stood beside him in the countless events and services they had all been part of. Men whose families he had entertained in his home, whose wives talked with his wife and whose children played together with his children, had all abandoned him, and some actively worked to murder him. One of them, Francois (name changed to keep the individual anonymous), a Hutu bishop, went so far as to refuse to leave Kigali until he was sure that Alphonse Karuhije was dead.

This man, Francois, continued to send men to seek Alphonse wherever he was hiding. Alphonse had locked himself in the church along with many of his parishioners. They hid in one of its many nooks and only went out if they were in dire need of food and other supplies. As the days and weeks raged on, he welcomed into the cathedral more and more people who came to seek sanctuary, believing that they were safe in a church. But across the nation, the Interahamwe, drunk with rage and blood were using churches as tombs, relying on the belief of thousands of Tutsis that the massacres would not breach the house of God. In a famous church in Bugesera in the Eastern Province, 5,000 men, women, and children were killed. In Nyakizu, 4,000 to 5,000 are said to have been murdered. Witnesses said that in Sainte-Famille Catholic Church in Kigali, the priest himself took arms against the Tutsis and led many who had sought refuge straight into the arms of their killers. Two thousand were killed there. In some instances, corpses five deep were stacked between aisles, some spilling over pews, and filled the stage where weeks prior choirs had stood worshipping. Other bodies lay upon the grass and church steps, some spread-eagled across the parking lot with their underwear pulled down, rape victims exposed to drive fear into survivors.

A HEAVENLY APPOINTMENT

As the horrific weeks pressed on and June approached, rumours began to surface of a strong surge from the RPF north and east of the country. Cautious optimism could be felt throughout the survivors hiding with Alphonse in the cathedral, but precautions still had to be made. The RTLM hosts slowly began to change their tune. Not even propaganda could hide what was apparent: the Rwandan armed forces and Interahamwe militia were losing. Many Tutsis were still being sought and killed, but the tide was now turning. As the RPF continued to gain more ground and made their way towards Kigali, many Hutus, fearing coming retribution, began to flee to Tanzania in the south, crossing Rusumo Falls.

Knowing that their time was running short, local Interahamwe in Kigali became more desperate to eliminate any remaining Tutsis in the city. It was around this time that they received a tip from Francois, who had caught a glimpse of Dad near the cathedral. A local group of Interahamwe were immediately deployed, and singing songs of murder they approached the cathedral. Their famous chants of "Let's do the work," which proceeded each massacre, were getting closer and closer.

Quickly the inhabitants hid in one of the two towers, shielding themselves with whatever they could find. From eyewitness accounts, we know that he was caught by the Interahamwe. And although it is impossible to tell what was happening in his mind as he was finally discovered, one can ascertain by the calmness and peace eye witnesses saw in him as he was marched out to die. "Inyenzi! Inyezi! You'd better hide, inyenzi; we are coming for you! Your God cannot save you, and neither can your man of God." Dad's heart would have probably stopped. The taunting and blasphemy he was used to, but what paralyzed him was their last sentence, "man of God." Not only did they know that he was in the area; they were coming for him. As he could hear the attackers scurrying below him, rummaging throughout the offices and sanctuary, flipping over pews, he would have silently continued to petition heaven. Peace would enveloped him every time he would utter the name of Jesus, a name whose power he intimately and experientially knew, but in silence, fear would creep back in. "Jesus. Jesus. Jesus." Thoughts of heaven would fill his soul as hymns and songs of praise flooded within. Such was the peace in that hiding place that he may not realize that he had been discovered and was being dragged along with the people he had rescued. His captors were drunk off violence, but he would be intoxicated in the sweet assurance that he would be Home soon.

Screaming, swearing, and sobbing ricocheted off the stone cathedral and its surrounding residences and buildings, amplifying the last desperate pleas by the discovered Tutsis, but my dad remained silent. Men, women, and children were lined up shoulder to shoulder, as behind them Interahamwe were quickly digging their grave. As they had been known to do, they began bartering with their captives, asking them if anyone was willing to purchase a bullet and exchange the cruelty of their machete for a swifter death. Then, from one side to the other, men, women, and children were stabbed, hacked, and shot, each falling like a domino, as the attackers approached your grandfather.

Many bodies surrounded him. Several feet behind him a large hole stood empty, like an open mouth waiting to be fed. Soon he would be in it. No one would be able to find his body, let alone identify it.

"Look at me!" Alphonse faced the yelling Interahamwe militia member who pointed an assault rifle at him. Others went back and forth, disposing of the slain bodies and searching for any Tutsis hiding in the brush. The man shouted insults and expletives and other words at him, but fear had rendered those words inaudible. So tangible was the overwhelming fear that no words could escape his mouth. Memories of his five children filled his mind. The two months since he last saw them was too long. David had only been two years old when he left them in Tanzania. Would he even remember his father? Or would he be the faceless one who had brought him into the world but was not around to help him navigate through it? He might never find out what happened to him, let alone understand it. *And Thacienne. My beautiful wife, Thacienne, what will become of you?* His family and their well-being were far more important to him than the circumstances he found himself in.

But wait. *What is this?* Peace descended upon his heart and mind. Fear lost its grip, and joy bubbled up from within him.

"Look at me, you filth!" The man was about to burst with hate. He spat in Alphonse's face, hit him with the blunt end of his assault rifle, and sent him staggering back, crying out in pain from a bleeding cut above his right eye.

Gathering himself, Dad stood upright and faced the man. The militia member stood petrified, with a look of confusion. Perhaps it was the peace and calm of Dad's face that caught him off guard, for the fearful, trembling man was no longer there, and in his place was a man of confidence.

The Bible says that before he died Stephen, the first martyr, "full of the Holy Spirit, gazed into heaven and saw the glory of God, and Jesus standing at the right hand of God" (Acts 7:55). From various reports of his departure that I heard, I believe that my father had a similar experience. His last words on this planet were "Hurry up, for the angels are waiting. We must not let them wait!"

Chapter 9
KINGDOM ABOVE THE CLOUDS

MOM PUT THE RECEIVER DOWN, SAT IN THE CLOSEST SEAT SHE COULD find, and gave in to the wave of emotion. Hot tears streamed down her face as she struggled to breathe. It had been months of waiting for a call, a letter, a messenger, or a vehicle that would bear her husband back to her. *Months? Was that all it was?* It seemed more like years. She had tried to get lost in her daily tasks, to stay busy and engaged.

Knowing there was a need for a Rwandese secretary in a Red Cross refugee camp nearby, she had applied for and had promptly been given a well-paying position. After RPF from neighbouring countries arrived in the rural areas of Rwanda, hundreds of thousands Hutu refugees fled the country and settled in Ngara, Tanzania, where the Red Cross had set up Benaco Refugee Camp. On April 30, 1994, 250,000 refugees crossed into Tanzania within twenty-four hours. UNHCR (the United Nations Refugee Agency in Canada) called it the largest and fastest refugee exodus in modern times. In almost a day, Ngara became Tanzania's second largest city.

Needless to say, it was a huge undertaking for the Red Cross, and they were looking for all the local help they could find. Because Mom was a Tutsi woman and the refugees in the camp included Interahamwe militias who had fled from fear of the vengeful force of the RPF, she was given an administrative role away from the camp. The stories she brought home were unforgettable.

Men and women who had participated in the brutality were now at the mercy of their consciences. Madness consumed them as the faces of those they had slain haunted their waking moments and ruled their sleep. The manifestations of their madness were things out of horror movies. Men would run out of their tents screaming that they were being eaten alive by babies. These were the baby killers. Others could be seen rolling on the ground, crying for water to quench their burning skin. These had killed with fire.

Mom thanked God that she was far away from it all, but she would come home from work hoping to hear news of Dad's welfare. Until now she had heard nothing. She recognized God's grace on her, helping shield our eyes and minds from what was taking place across the border and especially our dad's absence. The phone call she had just received from England finally brought some news.

During the genocide St. Mary's Church in the small market town of Newent in England displayed a poster of Mom, Dad, Patrick, Charity, and me as an aid to prayer. A powerful, peaceful vision had been revealed from heaven to a friend of our family. In the vision, my dad, on his knees, was encircled by a murderous horde trying to press through an invisible force field. Standing tall and strong behind Dad was a mighty angel, placing a crown on his head. According to this vision, told to my mother in the phone call, Dad was finally home.

I was eight years old when I was told that I would not see my father on this side again. I remember feeling a pause in time, as I was unsure of what I had just heard, and the uncontrollable weeping that followed when the full realization settled in. I also remember what happened next. A tangible peace wrapped around me, and a voice within caused me to snap to attention: "It will all be okay." Little did I know that it was the same embrace that my dad had experienced miles away in Rwanda.

RETURNING HOME

Africa is truly beautiful. One day I will take you there. Between Tanzania and Burundi flows Kagera River, part of the upper headwaters of the Nile. From Lake Rweru in Burundi in the south it flows north alongside the Rwanda-Tanzania border and over Rusumo Falls, a historical landmark in Rwanda, forming a great ravine that doubles as a natural border between the two countries. It was the scene of the first arrival of Europeans in Rwanda. Kagera River eventually works its way north to Uganda and eventually into the Nile.

During the genocide, Rusumo Falls became a place of extreme sadness and a renown killing place for the Interahamwe militia. By May of 1994, 10,000 bodies had been mutilated and thrown down the falls. Children skewered on sticks, carcasses with sawn off breasts and genitals, severed and dismembered limbs—all washed up on the shore, causing a hazard in Uganda's fishing market. At first, those fishing in that area were warned to thoroughly wash their catch, but by the latter part of the genocide, hardly anyone was buying fish. Wild animals attracted to the rotting flesh had begun feasting on the carcasses, causing even more danger for the region. Because water from almost every part of Rwanda drains into the Kagera River, those bodies were carried around the country. By June, 40,000 bodies had flown down the falls.

In November of 1994 we crossed Rusumo Falls and entered Rwanda. By then the RPF had fought their way through to Kigali and captured the city. The fleeing Interahamwe and Rwandan army were scattered in various refugee camps, blending with other refugees to evade capture and execution by the RPF. Most escaped into the Democratic Republic of Congo.

It was my first time entering Rwanda since leaving eight months before, but Mom had gone in weeks ahead to see if any family members had survived, perhaps holding hope that the one she was told was dead was still alive.

It had been a few months since the end of the genocide, and Rwanda was relatively safe. Many Tutsis who had fled were returning, looking for what of their former life had been spared. A few months before, Rwanda looked like something out of a Mad Max movie—a post-apocalyptic wasteland, but a jungle instead of the desert terrain of the Road Warrior. Ghost towns had become the dwelling places for vultures and other scavengers. Despite requests from RTLM broadcasts during the genocide to cover piles of bodies with banana tree leaves, corpses were everywhere. It was almost unreal. The bodies that littered villages and churches looked like broken dolls that an angry child had dismembered. Arms and legs lay several feet from the bodies they had belonged to. Perhaps stranger was the lack of a Third World staple, stray dogs, roaming alone or in packs. There were almost none to be found. RPF soldiers had put down dogs alongside Interahamwe militia. Accustomed to feeding on flesh, they had become even more dangerous and would attack soldiers and locals.

Mom had a driver take her around to places she knew, places once happy but whose walls now could tell inexplicable tales of violence. The only confirmation she had of Dad's death had been from a spiritual vision. Perhaps our friend had been mistaken or had misinterpreted the heavenly visitation. Some survivors had been reunited with their loved ones after all hope had been lost. Why not her? The odds were severely stacked against her. Seventy percent of all Tutsis had been killed. Yet hope has a way of evening the odds. As her driver approached the house, she saw him!

She commanded the driver to stop the car right away, jumped out, and ran up the porch stairs to the house, a house that was once hers, calling her husband's name. The man she thought was her Alphonse ran inside and shut the door. When Mom knocked, an irritated, unfamiliar family opened the door and asked who she was. With memories of her beloved filling her mind and anxiety in her voice, she tried to explain that it was her house they currently occupied and that she had seen who she thought was her husband walk in. And then her heart sunk as she saw the man she had presumed to be hers. He had been shirtless, working in the heat of the day, and seeing an unfamiliar woman approach, he rushed into the house to put on a shirt. Feeling a warm itch behind her eyes, she awkwardly apologized and excused herself.

She also went to the Kigali Cathedral where Dad served. Aided by the former archbishop of Canterbury, George Carey, who knew my father, she attempted to retrace his steps in order to locate his body, but she found nothing.

Twenty years later, Mom shared the heart-rending story with me. But she told it to me as an anecdote—a funny story, although then it was not. She had this light in her eyes that she never lost. I could see why my father had been drawn to her. Her spirit had remained strong and unjaded, even through what many would consider a cruel exercise in deferred hope. As the proverb goes, "Hope deferred makes the heart sick" (Proverbs 13:12). Yet as she observed the bones scattered about in the open and heard the stories of loss and terror, her hope was far from deferred. She was alive. Her children were alive. As far as she was concerned, God had kept His end of the bargain to her.

THE LUCKY ONES

The next time Mom returned to Rwanda, we were all with her. It would be the first time since we escaped that we would all be in Rwanda together as a family. We stopped in a village in Kibungo to see if there were surviving family members. As we got out of the car and entered the village centre surrounded by straw huts, an unnatural silence greeted us, as if we were standing in a sacred place. As I carefully maneuvered around the severed limbs and bones littered around the village floor, I felt and heard a crunch underneath my shoe, almost as if I had stepped on a shell of an ice cream cone. Looking down, I saw the skull I had trodden on with long grey hair sticking out from the crown, resembling that of an old woman. We found no one there.

Driving through the countryside, we could tell that things were much different from when we had left, yet not in a way you might have expected. To be sure, bodies and limbs were still being fished out of the river, and carcasses still lined rural streets and filled makeshift graves, but there was something else. If Rwanda had taken a deep breath before the genocide in preparation for what was coming, it was now breathing a sigh of relief. There was an air of freedom and jubilation. You could hear it in the songs that rose from villages that had once been overwhelmed with cries for mercy. Campfires around the country burned deep into the night as survivors exchanged stories of how they had outlived the days of slaughter. No one was a stranger in those days, only "lucky ones." Some areas were still deserted, and corpses were still found in many places, but for us they were emblems of a past that had passed.

MIRACLE IN BENACO

After unsuccessfully attempting to secure documents to return to England, we settled on going to Canada via Nairobi, Kenya, where churches were sponsoring refugee families from Africa. After we spent a few weeks in Kigali, the time came to leave for Kenya via Tanzania. After hours of driving on the rugged roads of the Tanzanian countryside, our sedan hit a massive pothole, destroying one of our tires. Crawling on ahead to see where we could stop to change the tire, we wandered into a trap.

By this time, the Great Lakes Refugee Crisis was in full effect. By the end of August of 1994, 2.1 million refugees were scattered in more than thirty-five camps around Rwanda's neighbouring nations. Although NGOs (non-governmental organizations) and the UN assisted in humanitarian efforts, many of the camps became militarized and politicized, and philanthropy was compromised as many relief organizations withdrew support.

Inside the camp, particularly the ones in Congo, cholera and other diseases broke out, and at one point the death toll was at 7,000 per week. At the camps that were built on a volcanic rock, it was impossible to dig mass graves, so the bodies of the diseased lined the side of the streets. The then US president Bill Clinton called it the worst humanitarian crisis in a generation.

In Ngara of the Kagera region of Tanzania, a place known for its farming and local crops, including bananas, passion fruit, papaya, and cassava, sat Benaco Refugee Camp. It had been set up to accommodate 200,000 refugees fleeing the genocide but was now climbing towards 600,000. The once lush countryside was no longer recognizable. Trees were being cut down at a rapid rate to sustain the masses, who needed firewood to cook their food. Even the sticks refugees during the early days of the camp had used to make crosses to mark the graves of the dead were stolen for firewood. Yards and yards of what looked like mud replaced the once grassy range. Yet a closer look would reveal the mud to be human feces. Despite the tireless work of the Red Cross and UN workers in making latrines available, it was difficult to keep up with the continually swelling numbers of refugees who arrived at the camp. As a result, many were defecating outside. The smell stung the eyes.

Worse yet, the camp was being run by fiefdoms of Interahamwe members who had blended into the escaping masses. As a result, moderate Hutus and Tutsis who wandered through the camp were being murdered at a rate of five per day. Local police, unable to maintain order, retreated from the camp, fearing an uproar, and instead boosted their force outside the camp perimeter to protect the local Tanzanian citizens. Slowly the camp began to spawn markets, barbershops, bike repair shops, and nightclubs as refugees took the aid rations supplied to them and sold them. At one point, a third of the rations going into the camp were being sold in the Tanzanian markets by refugees of Benaco.

Into this chaos we drove our Peugeot sedan, and the Rwandan licence plates were quickly spotted. A crowd began to form around our hobbled vehicle, while we did our best to press through the growing crowd on three tires. My frantic mother yelled from the passenger seat to put our heads down or else we would be discovered to be Tutsi. Peering through the back window, I saw men quickly approaching us, hoisting bloodstained machetes and peering through windows to catch a glimpse of who was inside. Suddenly a shout broke through the crowd—not an angry shout, but a jubilant one. With hands and machetes raised to the heavens, the crowd parted and cleared the way for us with applause!

As we cleared the area and drove on outside the camp on three tires, a group of local Tanzanian soldiers stopped us and helped us change our tires, perplexed about how we had made it out of the camp. It must have been that the people took more notice of the Rwandese plates than the occupants of the vehicle itself and in twisted patriotism cheered us through. Regardless, we had been saved once again.

HEAVEN'S TEST

Mom breathed a sigh of relief as we drove through the border and to our destination. Kenya would be our home for the next three years. It was the perfect place to regroup as a family and find out what the next plan would be, but unbeknownst to her, Mom was about to face her biggest test since Dad's departure.

We stayed in a countryside Methodist retreat centre, and it did not take long for friends and foes alike to discover that we had escaped unscathed from Rwanda. News began to travel that the Karuhije family had crossed the border into Kenya.

Mom was in the laundry room, trying to remove the greenish brown stains that had once again fastened themselves to the knees of my pants. No amount of scrubbing seemed to do the trick, and her frustration was almost at a boiling point as she thought of how many times in the past week she had chided us for roughhousing in the grass. But in secret she laughed to herself, thinking how good it felt to be angry about something so trivial.

The door creaked open. She glanced up from the sink as Charity waltzed in, announcing that some guests had come to see her. Trailing behind Charity were two men. The pants slid from her hands and dropped to the ground. She suddenly couldn't move.

Dad's betrayer, Francois, had heard the news of our escape, and I'm sure he had shared the same disbelief of others that we were not in some backwater refugee camp or lying in a bush somewhere, our bodies decomposing. We were in a comfortable and safe retreat centre with the freedom to rest, a privilege that had been denied most Rwandans, including him. As the RPF had begun their manhunt to bring to justice any perpetrators of the genocide, there was no rest for him. He had no doubt been looking over his shoulder lest he be identified, indicted, and sentenced, and every move would need to be calculated. But even he would have to witness the miracle that was our survival.

He pulled up with two of his friends to the Methodist retreat centre and instantly noticed Charity sitting on the cement stairs leading up to the main entrance, playing with a toy. *So it is true*, he must have thought. They inquired about her mother's whereabouts. Not knowing what this man had done, Charity innocently went to go look for our mom, who was in the laundry room. The men followed.

Our mother stared in shock at the man who had orchestrated the murder of her husband. Francois didn't know that she was aware of what he had done in ensuring her husband's death. During her first visit to Rwanda after the genocide, it was one of the first things she had inquired about, and no walls, trees, or soil could deny what had been unjustly done: Francois murdered him. He did not pull the trigger. He had done everything but. This is what was running through Thacienne's mind as he approached her with arms extended and a faux smile.

After some small talk where Thacienne gave confident, quick answers, the gentlemen turned to walk away. Their assignment had been to discover what Thacienne knew of their involvement, and they were confident she was unaware. Thacienne's steel nerves and inner prayer to God had done the trick, but deep inside she recognized a foreign sentiment brewing.

White heat, cold as ice, stung her heart and spread all over her body. It was as if the very hairs on her head were slowly rising in response to an electric current. It was the bitter root of unforgiveness, and it was manifesting in her physical body. *Why should that monster live after all that he has done? Hell is not hot enough for him.* Seething thoughts of anger swelled in her head, but a gentle wave washed over her heart and cooled the hatred. *Father, thank You for rescuing us and bringing us here. Forgive me for letting bitterness take over.* Her palms were sweating and her fists clenched, she noticed. She picked up the pants and tried to forsake the previous thoughts, but the seed of bitterness had been sown.

Years later, Mom would have a dream. By then the horrors and nightmares of the genocide in Rwanda seemed like a distant memory, but they were awoken that night. In her unconscious state she stood at a road, and a figure approached. As the stranger came into focus, she realized it was Francois. That bitter feeling began to form like the gathering of a storm, and in deep anger she screamed, "Francois, I hate you!" Francois stopped his advance suddenly, as if struck by an invisible force. Then he turned and walked away. Then, whether from conviction or pity, Mom called out to him, and as Francois turned around, from somewhere beyond herself, Mom said the words *I forgive you*. She woke up to a sense of peace and tranquility. The seed had been uprooted.

There would be no more words of hate or blame in our home towards anyone, regardless of how justified the words were. Unforgiveness and bitterness, which have been described as drinking poison in hopes that it will kill someone else, are the reason many do not experience all that God in His kingdom has for them. Had she held on to what she may have felt she had a right to hold on to, I shudder to think where I would be today. As impossible as it may seem to forgive the murderer of the one you love, it is a decision one must make regardless of whether the victimizer asks for it or not. Today, no ill will is held by anyone in my family for Dad's death, and none ever will be. Therefore, we are free.

MY MOTHER: INTERNATIONAL WOMAN OF MYSTERY

As support continued to pour in from friends and supporters around the world sympathetic to our escape and survival, we moved into Nairobi, Kenya's capital, and the children were promptly placed in school.

The apartment we moved into was in Sumo Flats, a gated community in a quiet neighbourhood in the city. It was perfect for us, being a safe area, as well as for its proximity to St. Christopher's Preparatory School, which we attended. A former ambassador in the Habyarimana administration was a neighbour, and he quickly became suspicious of us. While the refugee camps were filled with many families with similar stories to ours, we swam in the pool of a gated community, attended a private school, and had our own vehicle. *A Tutsi widow with five children? How could this be?* he must have thought. Thacienne had befriended a gentleman from the Rwandan embassy in Nairobi, who would come to visit occasionally, and when the former ambassador saw that man leaving our home and entering a vehicle with government plates, he was convinced that our mom was a spy for the RPF.

The facts were there and the suspicions valid, he thought; now all he needed was a crime. It came in the form of the murder of a Rwandan official in Kenya, and the former ambassador seized the opportunity and brought legal accusations against Mom. After being interviewed by police officers, she was to appear before the court as a suspect in a bogus murder charge.

Tension was high in Nairobi following the genocide, and many war masterminds had sought refuge in the large African nation. Some of them believed that Thacienne would turn them in unless she was dealt with. She appeared several times before the court, and the judge could not see a recently widowed mother of five being capable of the crime. The vast lack of evidence linking her to the murder reeked of bogus overreach. The case was promptly thrown out, and Mom was absolved from all accusations.

WINNIPEG

We began to understand that we would never be completely safe until we left Africa. England, being a safe place where Mom still had friends, was an obvious choice, but despite her every effort to gain entrance, all attempts continued to fail. Mom found herself on her knees yet again, praying to the One who had brought us there and who also had the power to take us someplace else.

I remember when my mom walked in with a postcard from a place in Canada called Winnipeg. *Golden Boy*, a statue of a boy holding a golden bundle of grain in his left arm and in his right hand a torch, was perched on the dome of the legislative building. Opposite the *Golden Boy* picture was a shot of beautiful green grass under a blue sky. I had heard of Canada but had no frame of reference for it. To our surprise and joy, Mom exclaimed that Winnipeg would be our new home. We celebrated that afternoon, not knowing what Winnipeg was but certain that if it was in North America, it may as well be called Paradise.

Chapter 10
THE END AND THE BEGINNING

IN THE HOSPITAL WITH MY MOTHER, I WOKE UP EARLY TO CATCH A flight back home to my wife in Vancouver. The visitors had all gone, and I had stayed the night in an undersized cot beside my mom's bed. Not wanting to wake her up, I leaned over to kiss her forehead, our trademark greeting, and her eyes opened to mine almost as if she expected it. As I looked at her I realized that the few weeks I would be away from her before seeing her again would be too long. My throat suddenly got a little dry, and a soft heat burned the back of my eyes. "Mom, I love you, and you are strong," I whispered to her.

I don't remember what she said to me; my mind was occupied with getting out of the room with my eyes still dry. I made it out in one piece, but as soon as I entered bustling hall of St. Boniface Hospital, not even the sunglasses I had on could stop the tears, which flowed down my cheeks and leaked from the bottom of the shades. The elevator could not come to the fifth floor fast enough.

The warm prairie morning sun blanketed me as I finally made it outside, still holding back the burst I was saving for the confines and shelter of the vehicle. I ran down the street and across the park to where my sister's car was parked, opened the door, and collapsed in the driver's seat. The thud of the door closing behind me gave me the liberty to finally let it all out.

I've often wondered whether the doctors and hospital staff who took care of her knew just who it was in their midst. There was no way Mom would talk about herself or what she had weathered. When Joanne, a close family friend, had taken her into emergency with early signs of the disease that afflicted her, a doctor came to collect her information. The doctor asked what her occupation was, to which Mom replied, "foster parent." By that time, all of us children had left the house, and the four children she was fostering became another avenue for her to minister the love of Jesus through. Yet even we had warned her of the toll it was taking on her to be a mother again at that stage in her life to four children under the age of twelve. But stopping fostering would be akin to giving up a part of her heart, and she would have none of it. She loved those kids. Perhaps she felt responsible for them on a much deeper level than another foster family would. Their biological mother had been forced to give them up, as she could no longer take care of them. She had birthed ten kids, all before her thirtieth birthday. My mother, who became a social worker after arriving in Canada, had witnessed a broken system that was unable to properly fulfill the needs of children, so she had taken the four kids in. She felt a duty to teach them about Jesus and raise them up to be different in the world. Even after she was admitted to the hospital and her body continued to break down under the tumour and treatment, she constantly asked about her foster kids and if they were in a good home.

So when she had replied only that she was a foster parent, it was not self-deprecation on her part; she had embraced this chapter in her life and saw privilege in it. Joanne, who also knew the doctor who was asking, would have none of it. "She is not just a foster mom, doctor; this woman is a survivor of the Rwanda genocide. She lost her husband but brought her five children out. She is...royalty."

I'll never forget an answer Mom gave some hospital staff who came to share their insights on her diagnosis. With all the tact and sensitivity they could muster they looked at her and said, "Thacienne, this is a nasty, aggressive cancer."

Unflinchingly, and with the defiance of a woman whose life had been threatened once or twice, she replied, "And we will be nasty and aggressive in prayer." And this summed up my mom's most recent encounter with something that was trying to rob her of her life. She would often say, "I've survived two genocides, and I'll survive this." Her faith and strength became an inspiration throughout the hospital and beyond as many shared her story. I'll never forget the faces of the grief counsellors, doctors, and nurses, who must have thought we were in denial every time they mentioned the word "terminal" to us. We just stared at them unfazed, my mom on the hospital bed leading the brave front. As Job 5:22 says, "At destruction and famine you shall laugh, and shall not fear the beasts of the earth."

But it was more than a brave front. There are some who have stared at death square in the eye and uttered defiantly,

"I'm not afraid of you." My father, Alphonse, was one of those, and my mom was cut from the same cloth. Far from denial, they had their eyes set on another world and another hope, where a King sits, having triumphed over sickness and diseases and fear. Thacienne's hope was in that King, that same person who had saved her life many times before.

As time went on, it became more and more apparent that that King might be calling her home to a hero's welcome, she having perhaps completed her task on earth. As more and more of her physical strength failed and her speech went from whispers to silence, one of her greatest features, her eyes, became the only source of communication, along with a slight head nod or shake. One morning I realized that her eyes were darting back and forth around the room, zooming past the family who sat around her. I approached her and whispered to her, asking her if she could see "others" in the room, motioning to indicate angels. Her eyes locked on mine, and she nodded ever slightly in the affirmative.

Even then, Mom fought to live and was convinced that she had more to do in this world. But on November 26, 2014, Thacienne Mukaminega's body sat as an empty shell in a beautiful casket before the hundreds who attended her funeral, but my mom was no longer there. As her children and her friends came forward to eulogize her, the theme remained constant, no matter who was speaking: royalty. The congregation sat spellbound and misty-eyed as we recounted her story and legacy.

The young Thacienne who had stared at her house burning to the ground five decades earlier was now standing with the King who had protected her, Jesus.